Advance Praise for *Make Magic of Your Life*

"A mini-masterpiece from a true modern mage. While showing you how to *make magic your life*, Thorn Coyle succeeds delightfully in demonstrating how to *make your life magic*."

—Lon Milo DuQuette, *author of Enochican Vision Magick and Understanding Aleister Crowley's Thoth Tarot*

"What can you do with magic? Everything and T. Thorn Coyle proves that in her book *Make Magic of Your Life: Purpose, Passion, and The Power Of Desire*. Through the use of the framework of the elemental Four Powers of the Magus, sometimes known also as the powers of the Sphinx or the Witches' Pyramid, she guides and encourages readers to step into their power and thereby into their sacred work. The chapters weave back and forth between highly spiritual matters and practical actions in the world. By the time you reach the end of the book, you have a sense of how to remain present and aware in all the worlds and all the arenas of action that comprise your life. It is a book about transformation that is both outward and inward and accessible to people from a wide range of spiritual backgrounds. It is just as valuable for a practitioner of magic as it is for the general public. I strongly encourage groups and individuals to add this book to their list of worthy books."

—Ivo Dominguez, Jr., author of *Casting Sacred Space: The Core of All Magickal Work* and a Wiccan Elder in the Assembly of the Sacred Wheel

"If you're longing to reawaken your soul's calling and dive into the life of your highest vision, read this book and keep it close by for the journey! Imbued with a fierce magical essence, Thorn Coyle's work is unmatched in its unique and straightforward approach to finding and manifesting your heart's desire."

—Satya Colombo, author of *Flo Fierce*

D1232426

MAKE
MAGIC
OF YOUR
LIFE

MAKE

MAGIC

OF YOUR

LIFE

MAKE
MAGIC
OF YOUR
LIFE

PURPOSE, PASSION,
AND THE POWER
OF DESIRE

T. THORN COYLE

WEISERBOOKS
San Francisco, CA / Newburyport, MA

First published in 2013 by Weiser Books

Red Wheel/Weiser, LLC
With offices at:
665 Third Street, Suite 400
San Francisco, CA 94107

ISBN: 978-1-57863-538-2

Cover design by Jim Warner
Cover photograph © Circe Invidiosa, 1892 (oil on canvas), Waterhouse, John William (1849-1917) The Bridgeman Art Library

Printed in the United States of America

Bill Moyers: Unlike heroes such as Prometheus or Jesus, we're not going on our journey to save the world but to save ourselves.

Joseph Campbell: But in doing that you save the world. The influence of a vital person vitalizes, there's no doubt about it. The world without spirit is a wasteland. People have the notion of saving the world by shifting things around, changing the rules, and who's on top, and so forth. No, no! Any world is a valid world if it's alive. The thing to do is to bring life to it, and the only way to do that is to find in your own case where the life is and become alive yourself.

FROM THE PBS SERIES, *THE POWER OF MYTH*

CONTENTS

MAKE
MAGIC
OF YOUR
LIFE

MAKE
MAGIC
OF YOUR
LIFE

CHAPTER O
STARTING THE JOURNEY

*Some say the shards of the cosmos were created from desire: a
desire to know, a desire to feel, a desire to become something
new. Some say that the Limitless, the Great Zero, the
All—sometimes called God Hirself, or by many other
names—divided for the sake of Love, to better know Hirself.[1]
Some others say it was just time for a change.*

*Some say that things exploded from the heat of this
desire.*

*They say, as time stretched, becoming linear, some things
moved farther and farther apart while others drew themselves back together, forming new shapes, different colors, or
strange and beautiful harmonies that became new notes al-
together. Some say we can do this, too. Our unique sparks remember their connection to the whole. We can follow the great
star Desire, and join the cosmos in dancing forth creation. We*

---

1. "Hir" is a genderless pronoun. "God Hirself" is a way of naming the
   unnameable flow of non-duality, sometimes experienced as the fabric
   of everything. I experience both connection and multiplicity, often
   calling myself a "non-dualist and polytheist."

create worlds with our lives, our loves, our visions, work, and joy.

What is stretching out inside of you? What in your soul longs for reconnection? What feels the greatness of unfolding Mystery when you gaze upon a marigold, or look up at the stars? What in you might explode in a brilliant rush of heat and light?

Follow that . . .

We cannot know the outcome of our actions, but sometimes we must act anyway. We don't know the impact of this word, or that thought. We can choose carefully and aim with all our skill, but we still cannot know what winds may blow, affecting the trajectory of our intentions. Magic, no matter how clearly planned, includes elements of chance. That is the beautiful surprise of cocreation.

To work magic is to dare. Finding our Divine Work in the world is a chance to risk what feels known. We must learn to trust intuition, and listen to the longing in our souls. To find your soul's work, follow your heart's desire.

Ancient peoples of the North spoke of *wyrd*. Some translate this word as "fate," but I prefer to name it "destiny." Fate is most often seen as something completely out of our hands, but my view of reality is this: *We weave the strands of destiny with the multiverse.* We take what is, what has been, and what shall be, and weave in strands of longing, will, and intention. We take risks of our own making, rather than wandering helplessly along. In fully acknowledging that we are cocreators of this world, we take our lives into our own hands, weaving our will into the fabric of being. Ours are not the only threads that make the pattern of the world we live in, but they are just as necessary as all the rest.

Will you dare to take up the magic that is your life? Will you answer the call of the cosmos to your heart and soul?

THE CALL

Your life is shaped by the end you live for. You are made in the image of what you desire.

THOMAS MERTON

There you are, living your life, when suddenly, the call comes. Perhaps you were avoiding it, or perhaps you hoped it would show up someday. Once you hear the call, what do you do? Will you give in to resistance, or step bravely toward the fire burning at your core?

I call myself a magic worker, having studied spirituality, magic, and ritual arts for most of my life. Along with writing and teaching, I have also worked with many spiritual-direction clients one on one. Over many years' time, I've seen other magic workers—as well as ministers, activists, computer programmers, and single parents—struggle with manifestation and sometimes actively refuse to make magic for themselves. They feel too timid to do so, as though asking for what they want and taking action to get it were beneath the purview of their spirits or too selfish an undertaking. I watched this with astonishment and finally realized that these clients and students struggled with the calling of desire.

I get notes via email and social media from strangers all over the world asking things like this:

I hear "do the things you love and you will find the one" or something to that effect. It makes sense to me. The question that I cannot readily answer is how do you truly know or find the things that you really love? Sounds simple and for some people it is easy. For some if us, it is not.

No. It often isn't simple. Self-help gurus can tend toward the glib and forget how hard it can be. We can also get caught up in thinking that our purpose needs to be some earth-shattering thing. Most often, the soul's work is what feels most ordinary to each of us.

One factor that contributes to denying our powers of creativity and manifestation is that the purveyors of "The Secret" have told us to "think our way" toward riches, forgetting that we all create this world together—artists, teachers, creators of toxic waste, rivers, drivers of cars, tall trees, builders of nuclear power plants, manta rays, lovers, ravagers of rain forests, mountain gorillas, users of cell phones, doctors, dragonflies, and friends. We become afraid to manifest because we think it means to desire good things only for ourselves—setting money or big houses ahead of purpose, service, and connection, and blaming misfortune on the thoughts of those afflicted.

This realization caused me to take a step back in order to re-examine my own forays into magic. I had to look again at my processes. How had I worked to heal my soul from the curse of unworthiness or feelings of selfishness or actual self-centeredness? I remember having to stop doing magic and making prayers that were ineffective stabs at some perfect life to assess who I truly was, and to start making magic based around the tugging I had always felt in my heart and soul. To do this, I had to face knowing myself on even deeper levels than I had previously allowed. I had to drop the mask of knowing it all, of being competent, and admit that there was a lot I did not know—about myself, about relationships, money, and love, about conflict and deeper service, and about the world.

So many of us end up trapped in boxes of emotion and mind that are too small to live in well. I certainly did. We fear that to desire is to be self-centered or greedy in the midst of a world in need. We settle for being "kind of good enough" instead of thriving. When we engage in these behaviors, the soul's spark dims and we grow less able even to sense what our Divine Work is, let alone share it with the world.

We simultaneously long for and fear the fruits of desire. I have seen magic workers afraid to manifest, and warriors too beaten down and exhausted to fight for what they loved most deeply. My heart went out to these people. Trying to answer their questions led to a series of blog posts, an online class, and, finally, this book.

By listening to the work that was being put in front of me, I realized that it was time to get to the root of what impedes our magic and the soul's work. If Merton was right, and desire shapes our lives, it was time for me to take steps toward realizing, courting, and manifesting desire.

THE FOUR POWERS OF THE SPHINX

To attain the SANCTUM REGNUM, in other words, the knowledge and power of the Magi, there are four indispensable conditions—an intelligence illuminated by study, an intrepidity which nothing can check, a will which cannot be broken, and a prudence which nothing can corrupt and nothing intoxicate. TO KNOW, TO DARE, TO WILL, TO

KEEP SILENCE—such are the four words of the Magus, inscribed upon the four symbolical forms of the sphinx.

ELIPHAS LÉVI[2]

We will explore our sense of purpose by following desire through the magical Four Powers of the Sphinx written of by Kabbalist and magician Eliphas Lévi: To Know, To Will, To Dare, and To Keep Silence. Controversial mage Aleister Crowley added a fifth power: To Go. For me, the fifth power is To Manifest—a quality that states that, over time, we can bring the Four Powers together into a whole, sparking the soul's purpose into a fully active state, enabling us to share our gifts with the world.

What Lévi calls the Holy Kingdom—the *Sanctum Regnum*—rests within the heart of our own souls. It is the place where we reign, complete unto ourselves. To claim sovereignty over our individual kingdoms is to step fully into our Divine Work, becoming cocreators of the unfolding cosmos. This is often called The Great Work; it is the deep soul purpose to which we can all aspire. This need not feel earth-shattering—although it may. It just has to belong to us. The steps toward it begin with desire kindling within us. Without worrying about what our purpose is right now, we can begin with desire in its quieter forms: the pull toward art, settling onto a meditation bench, the study of healing, the gaze of love, the wish to serve.

I encourage you to allow your soul to sink into that purpose; let your body open to that purpose. Give yourself that gift.

---

2. From *Transcendental Magic* (Kessinger Publishing, 1942). Later annotated editions are available.

APPROACHING THE SPHINX

Lévi's Sphinx represents the coming together and rebalancing of disparate elements. Sphinxes appear in many cultures; they act as guardians, challengers, and dispellers of harm.[3] How these elements are represented varies from culture to culture, although all sphinxes have human heads and animal bodies. The Sphinx Lévi writes about has the head of a man, the forepaws and shoulders of a lion, the wings of an eagle, and the flanks of a bull. The Sphinx Lévi writes about has the head of a man, the forepaws and shoulders of a lion, the wings of an eagle, and the flanks of a bull. The soaring height of the eagle provides the shift in mental perspective that transforms information into something more — To Know. The lion represents the ability to live in pride and claim the power of our intention—To Will. The human is the cup bearing Aquarius, who shows us that we hold the vessel said to represent the heart, our courage —To Dare. The bull is solid strength, and the ability to be still and to guard the Mystery —To Keep Silence.[4]

To approach the Sphinx is to acknowledge that we are ready for our lives to change.

At each stage in life, we get a chance to dig more deeply into our hearts and souls, to move closer to unlocking the Sphinx's

---

3. Those qualities come from Egypt, Greece, and East Asia respectively.

4. The attributes of the beings that make up the sphinx shift depending on who is writing about it. Even the order of the Four Powers has changed over time, settling on To Know, To Will, To Dare, and To Keep Silence in contemporary practice. This corresponds with the elemental sequence of Air, Fire, Water, and Earth. For Lévi, the elemental sequence was Fire, Water, Air, and Earth. What matters is that we remain consistent within our own system and know that all systems are just routes to the Mystery that cannot properly be mapped or set into code.

riddle. We get to dare all over again. And while this isn't a book on magic per se, studying this book will help to increase the amount of magic in our lives until, over time, they become continuous acts of magic. In other words, we can make magic of our lives. We can solve the mystery of the Sphinx.

Embedded here are theories and meditations—soul support—to guide us into a fuller relationship with desire. We will find where we are on the journey and whether we are masters or neophytes at following desire. We will come to know that each stage of life includes a place to start fresh in our apprenticeship and requires a different one of the Four Powers—a calling up of bravery, a mustering of will, the gathering of implements, settling into the cadences of what each day brings. There is a large arc of life that holds smaller arcs within. That is why I often hear clients or students say: "But haven't I dealt with this already?" They have—at age sixteen or thirty-six or sixty.

The more we realize that the whole cosmos is in process, the better able we are to follow our own flow, to forgive our mistakes, celebrate our successes, and recommit to our purpose. Consistently successful people find ways to commit to themselves and their desire on a daily basis. Everything they do—work, rest, play, spiritual practice—supports their desire, whether they've named it or not. They realize that to live happy, healthy, sustainable lives, they need to follow through on their commitments to themselves. We can learn to do the same.

To help in this process, I have included action items at the end of each chapter that give instructions on how to do the work of the Four Powers as you move through them. Along the way, we will also be blessed with the thoughts and words of some people who successfully navigate the pathways of desire. This Wise Council of authors, entrepreneurs, social workers, activists, doctors, musicians, and teachers shares insights into how they stay the course. I recommend that you take this book one chapter at a time and give yourself *at least* one week to let the meditations sink in and to work through the action items that will support your deepening.

This book also contains stories from spiritual-direction clients, students, and friends. These are markers on the path, and illustrations of both challenges and possibilities. I also felt it necessary to disclose some of my own stories, to show how the material in this book has affected my life. All the theory here is rooted in practice, both mine and others'.

If all you do is read this book cover to cover, you may get some things out of it. More than likely, however, it will become just another experience that briefly inspires your thoughts or emotions, but then leaves you in search of the next book, the next workshop, or the next teacher. As one long-term student said: "There is no easy pass." The only way through is to engage your body, mind, and heart. The only way through is to face the Sphinx, to seek out the deeper questions, and to do the work.

THE QUEST

My own quest to manifest my soul's desire has encompassed my life thus far. Sometimes I've felt as if I were following a thread; at other times, it was as if a strong rope pulled me forward. I have had to make difficult choices in order to keep listening to the longing of my soul.

The secret is that, when we follow this longing, we follow a deeper and broader truth. We cannot know how the cycles will play out. Marriages may form or dissolve. Jobs may come and go. Friendships may be tested and strengthened. Through it all, if we keep listening, choosing, and showing up with as much presence as we can muster, desire will unfold in strong and surprising ways.

I cannot know the effects my choices will have on the lives of others. Sometimes this feels wrenching; I've had to do a lot of soul-searching in order to continue. But this, too, is part of the process of desire—of coming to know the mystery of the Sphinx. We learn to listen more deeply, on every level. Hopefully, we learn greater trust of our hearts and souls.

My quest has always included Lévi's power To Dare. The consequences of daring can be difficult, but also fruitful. Take heart. Offer love to the world. Offer love to your soul. Offer love to your own life, unfurling like a tender vine soon to bear a new and fragrant flower.

Soul Support

What does desire feel like in your body? Does it coil in your belly or cause your heart to thump or your sex to contract and then open? Are you poised for movement or ready to lie down and receive? What scent is carried on the wind when you think of desire? Is it magnolia blossoms, or simmering soup? Amber or wood smoke or freshly laundered sheets? The crackling of ozone or the scent after rain? What does desire taste like? Elderflower cordial or fresh blackberries, warm from the sun? Kale cooked in olive oil, or chocolate cake with whipped cream? What does desire sound like? Laughter, the deep voice that rises from your belly? The calling of ravens in high desert? Or the pounding of waves upon the shore? Find these. Follow these. Let your searching be informed by the power of desire.

MAKE MAGIC OF YOUR LIFE

THE POWER OF DESIRE

Each one of us has a fire in our heart for something. It's our goal in life to find it and to keep it.

MARY LOU RETTON

When I tell people I'm writing about desire, their responses vary. Some assume I am only talking about sex. Others' eyes light up with interest. Still others become confused—doesn't desire cause suffering? Some grow wistful, as if desire felt very far away.

Desire harnesses life energy so that we can move forward into what my core tradition calls The Work of This God, which can be interpreted as our purpose or destiny.[5] This is the idea that there is some work—some practice, joy, or way of being—that only we can manifest in this world. This may sound like a platitude, but it is a statement that I find to be deeply true. Without desire, we can languish in our lives, never dedicating ourselves to the practices that will point us toward our Divine Work.

I like to look at the parts of the self that want to reject the idea of a life purpose or the soul's work and ask "Why?" Is there anger present? Or cynicism or a sense of betrayal? Or a fear of things not working out? There often is. But we can invite our fears, anger, or cynicism to the table of desire. They add spice and savor—cinnamon and chili—to our dark chocolate.

If we each have our own soul work—if we are *all* special— what does that mean? It means that we each have work that is of utmost importance—and so does everybody else. This means that, while our expressions of life power may be different, there is a sameness to us as well. We share common ground and common experience. We are special and, in many ways, we are just like

---

5. This is known in some traditions as "True Will."

everyone else. This realization has helped to keep me in balance. It helps me avoid denigrating my own contribution, yet keeps me from elevating it above another's.

In Chuck Palahniuk's *Fight Club*, Tyler Durden states: "You are not a beautiful and unique snowflake. You are the same decaying organic matter as everyone else, and we are all part of the same compost pile." This is true. It is simultaneously true that everything in the compost pile starts out looking and tasting different, and that each thing brings a different nutrient to the process. We do not start off as compost; we start off as this flower, or that piece of fruit, or a tasty bread baked by an artisan. Yes, we end up as the same stuff; and yes, we even begin with similar components. But that does not take away the fact that, in our differences, there is beauty. He dances; she sings; he parents; she plants. All of this is necessary to the healthy functioning of the biosphere—or more largely, what I call the cosmosphere or the metaphoric garden of God Hirself.

In seeking our souls' desire, we have the opportunity to see our deepest selves. In manifesting our will in the world, we take our places as cocreators of the cosmos, as true denizens and full participants of this gorgeous earth.

DESIRE AS LOVE

Just as a water molecule in a raindrop is ultimately drawn to the ocean, one way or another, no matter how long it takes and how many incarnations it must go through, so too is awareness drawn to its source. Kabbalists say that love operates in the same way. Love is based on a yearning for

completion: to be whole, to be in harmony, to be connected,
and to be free.

RABBI DAVID A. COOPER[6]

Rabbi Cooper is talking here about the power of love. The ancient Pagan Greeks spoke to this quite clearly: the soul's longing to return to a state of pure connection is directed by *eros*.

We tend to think of the erotic as something that has to do only with sexual titillation. The erotic *does* deal with sex, but with sex in a far more expansive sense then our over-culture presents. *Eros* is the sexual impulse that moves the planets around the sun, draws the drop of water to the river, and—more important for the Greeks—draws the soul back to its source.

Desire is the heart's wish for deep fulfillment. The completion Rabbi Cooper writes of is the integration of ourselves as humans, doing our Divine Work in the world. To be complete is not to become static. To be complete is to have realized that our deeper purpose is to live in harmony with the field of life that is God Hirself. We are enacting our destiny as surely as the stars enact their own.

To me, this underscores the need to include as much of myself as possible when connecting to desire. If my mind resists—or if my sex shuts down, or my body refuses, or my emotions get stuck in fear—it is all the more difficult to feel that which calls me. We are being drawn inexorably toward our deepest selves, and our deepest selves are connected fully to the whole cosmos. God Hirself is within us.

---

6. From *God Is a Verb: Kabbalah and the Practice of Mystical Judaism* (Riverhead, 1998).

Soul Support

Slow down your breathing. Feel the edges of your skin. Take a deep breath and gather all of your attention into a shining ball inside your head. As you exhale, imagine that ball descending, coming to rest just a few inches above your pelvic cradle. Just outside your skin, imagine concentric fields of energy connecting you to the space around you. Breathe in again and, as you exhale, imagine those energy fields opening, softening, and relaxing.

Now, breathe in again; imagine breath moving in through your sex and out through every pore of your skin. Try it again, this time physically squeezing your perineum or vaginal walls. Release the muscles as you exhale. Do this six to nine times. On your last exhalation, tilt your head back and breathe up.

Allow your attention to return to your core, just above your pelvis. Ask yourself: "What do I desire?" Be open to the answer in any form. It may come as a feeling, a sense on your skin, an emotion, a thought, a sound, or an image. Don't tense up. Allow yourself to relax further, opening to desire. Even if you cannot yet name it, know that desire is present. It is always present. Each moment you are alive, something inside of you wishes to connect.

Feel love pour down over your head—a blessing from the cosmos, a kiss from God Hirself.

Stay here for as long as you like. Then, breath by breath, bring yourself back. Drink some water. Write in your journal. Sing. Dance. Paint. Do whatever moves you.

THE TUG OF DESIRE

I bet God that if I lived, I would try to find out the vague directions whispered in my ears and find the road it seemed I must follow.

ZORA NEALE HURSTON

As we live our lives, something often tugs at us. We want something out of life, whether or not we are certain what that is. For many of us, the tugging begins in simple ways: a want, a need, or a strange feeling that something is missing. Others get the lightning bolt of realization. Regardless of how desire arrives, what we do next says a lot about our conditioning and personality, and our relationship with ourselves. Do we seek out this want? Do we try to figure out what may be missing? Do we bury the feeling with a sense of practicality or a conviction that somehow we do not deserve happiness, adventure, or anything out of the ordinary? Do we muffle the sound of the call, or unstop our ears and learn to listen with every fiber of our being?

The tugging we feel can manifest itself in adolescent rebellion, in the classic "midlife crisis," or in myriad other ways. We can choose to listen more deeply to this longing and find forms of self-expression that are not just ways to break free at any cost, but ways to invest in our souls' unfolding and our hearts' desire. Do we really want to react against what life has given us, or do we want to take the time and put in some extra effort to choose, actively, what we really want? Reaction is not good enough. It won't really bring the happiness, fulfillment, or autonomy we seek. We can learn to claim, to act, to say "Yes!"

We are called to move from what feels ordinary into living the extraordinary. This will look and feel different for each of us, which makes this *our* journey and no one else's. There is no other person's life or experience to which we can compare our own. We are distinct stars in the firmament. To deny this is to deny desire, destiny, and our Divine Work. Does this mean that we live our lives in a vacuum, unaffected by everything around us? Certainly not. The beauty of the sky exists in the interplay of darkness with the varying points of light, and with the relationships the stars form with each other, knowingly or not. We can all be stars in constellation if we wish it. And, in any case, we all serve to form the fabric of the sky.

Do you hear the calling of your soul to adventure? This is the first step on your own heroic journey.

REDEFINING SUCCESS

Success is liking yourself, liking what you do, and liking how you do it.

MAYA ANGELOU

There is plenty of success to go around, just not the sort of success we may have been taught to value. When we redefine success to be more in line with our desire, we begin to redefine our relationship to what I call the over-culture, to sustainability, and to the ideas of scarcity and abundance.

Love and creativity are renewable resources. Other resources are scarcer—fear and ignorance create systems of injustice and devastation that can make us feel alone, angry, bewildered, or like failures. An internal feeling of scarcity and panic constricts the flow of life and limits our relationship to the processes of the cosmos. Yes, there is external scarcity. Yes, some resources are finite. Yes, sometimes we feel so beaten down or overwhelmed that even

MAKE MAGIC OF YOUR LIFE

access to creativity and love feels limited. I feel compassion for this. I also know that we have to find a way, somehow, to try.

If those of us who live in relative privilege act as if love and creativity are scarce, how much more is required of a person living in grinding poverty, or a war zone, or some other place where systems of fear and ignorance hold sway? Fear and ignorance are everywhere, but they do not have to define how we live or who we are. And they certainly do not have to define how we assign value.

I value the desire for love, beauty, engagement, and success. For me, success is the sense that I contribute to the world and, in turn, receive love and satisfaction. Some may fight against this, saying: "I work so hard, but I don't feel love!" Take a breath and consider for a moment the ways that a perception of love as a scarce resource may have closed you down. The more we expand, open, and loosen our grip on anger, fear, or resentment, the less control these feelings will have over love's flow. With the flow of love, the simplest things can make us feel as if we are rich. Sunlight on leaves. Clean water. Kindness.

Some of my friends struggle hard, with scarcity dogging their heels and a cacophony of messages shouting in their eyes and ears: "Just do it!" "There is nothing you can't do!" "Everything is possible if you just try hard enough!" "What are you waiting for?" "The time is now!" "Here are my five simple steps to success!" On and on. Partial truths. Halfway inspiration. Sometimes these are attempts to fight against the small voice that says: "But what if there really *isn't* enough to go around?" And that voice is partially true as well. There isn't enough gold or oil or food or clean water—at least not at the rates we are using them and not with our current relationship to the earth and each other. But we have the ability to change this—not to increase the resources themselves, but to shift our relationship to them in such a way that we can share better. So here we are, back to the need to redefine success and to return to our stores of creativity and love.

What would it be like if we did not all need to own cars or washing machines? What would it be like if we made music together again? What would it be like if we pooled our ideas and our time? What would it be like if we all slowed down? What would it be like if we used less, bought less, and instead paid a fair price in exchange for knowing that others were getting a fair wage for their labor? What would it be like if we collectively valued the teaching of children more than the stockpiling of gold? What would it be like if we remembered that success is not a static state, but a process that ebbs and flows, shaping the shore and always returning to the vastness of the ocean?

We would be able to follow our desire with curiosity and joy. We would know success.

Soul Support

What does your soul desire? Where do you feel constricted? How can changing your definition of success help bring you ease? What changes in the values of the over-culture may become possible if you believe in yourself enough to follow your desire to fruition? A sense of scarcity and constriction inside does not help to alleviate any real patterns of scarcity outside.

Find the places where tension or fear resides in your body. Take a breath. Relax. Expand. Once again, find the stillness that rests just above your pelvic bowl. Regroup around this center; drop your attention into it on a breath. Listen to your soul.

Now notice the space around you. How much space are you willing to take up? Imagine that, right now, you can inhabit your body and the field around you fully, extending out two to three feet. This is your circumference, your aura edge, where your energy meets and penetrates everything around you.

Breathe into the stillness at your center. Exhale out to the edge of the field of your shining body. Know your center. Know your circumference. Breathe into both every day.

If you feel constricted, inhale into stillness, then exhale and let your breath push your edges outward, giving all of your parts more room to breathe.

THE TEMPLE OF DESIRE

We dance in the heat of our heart's desire . . . open the gate,
the key is within, to the temple of the heart.

FROM MY SONG, "HEART'S DESIRE"[7]

When we are able to redefine success, we arrive at the threshold of the Temple of Desire. The more open we become to desire, the more we learn its ways and allow our relationship to it to open, the more it will infuse each moment. When we reach the place where our lives are suffused with the power of desire, when each choice we make is a confirmation of this relationship, our longing ceases. We no longer feel the yawning need that haunted our first forays into desire's hot touch. We feel well-fed, with desire our long-time companion on life's journey. We will still make mistakes, but

---

7. Available on *Songs for the Strengthening Sun* at *http://thorncoyle.bandcamp.com.*

overall we will feel whole in ways we may never have thought possible. We will have reached a place, not of apathy or detachment, but of the certainty that life is as it is, because that in itself is a gift. Our presence—our lives, our work, our love, our pain, our laughter—is the gift we receive in return. This great exchange builds the world, lights up the cosmos, and kindles a small flame inside every being we encounter. We will have arrived, yet there is no place to arrive at. We will be moving with the holy dance of life.

That may feel very far off for most of us. Some may feel bogged down with responsibilities or worries about family, work, school, or health. Some may simply feel confused. Others may have noticed the tugging of desire and may feel that they are on their way. Wherever you are in this journey, let worry go right now. Take a big breath and release it on a sigh.

Then find that within you that is willing to step forward. Approach the threshold of the Temple of Desire.

Soul Support

Within each of us is a Temple of Desire. Follow its fragrance. Feel the tugging at your solar plexus, your heart, your sex, or your mind. Where is that center inside of you today? Where is your connection to desire? Find it in your body. Feel its resonance. Does it feel strong or barely present today? Pause. Breathe. Notice. Open the soles of your feet. Open the palms of your hands. Open the top of your head. Breathe into the silent still place in the center of your belly. Breathe from the soles of your feet to the crown of your head. Begin to dance.

MAKE MAGIC OF YOUR LIFE

Action

1. Find your connection to divinity. Is this a connection to the flow of All, a connection with God Hirself? Is there a specific deity who is stepping forward to help you with this work? Listen. Build an altar. Make an offering to this deity, or to your own connection with the Limitless Divine, and know that this work you embark upon is also an offering to yourself and to the world.

2. Take on the task of examining and being with your breath. Notice when you hold your breath; notice when your breath quickens; notice how often you breathe deeply. Every morning, take five minutes to slow your breathing, to deepen your breath, to relax the tensions that impede the flow of breath. Allow yourself simply to sit and breathe, beginning your day in a place of relative quiet. Opening to breath will eventually open you to the flow of desire. Desire requires access to energy, and ends up feeding energy. Energy is fed by breath.

3. Practice the center and circumference work on pages 20–21 every morning. Get used to connecting to the stillness just above your pelvis as you inhale; and send an exhalation out to define the edges of your energy field, also known as your aura. Do this in the morning, and then as many times a day as you remember. All other practices can flow to and from this.

PART I

To Know

WE ASK THE WISE COUNCIL:[8]

WHEN DID YOU FIRST FEEL THE TUGGING OF YOUR HEART'S/SOUL'S DESIRE?

Probably playing with toys when I was a baby. And almost every day since. See—I think it's dangerous to think in terms of "heart's desire" because it sounds like such a huge overwhelming thing. (If you think love needs to look like Romeo and Juliet, you'll overlook a great relationship that grows slowly.) So instead, I try to notice the very subtle tugs about what excites me and what scares me on a small moment-to-moment level.

DEREK SIVERS

8. For more information on our wise counselors, please see page 233 at the end of this book.

It was August 1979. I had left my job as a systems engineer in London six years before and returned to Australia. I'd moved into the bush in northern NSW and helped build a Buddhist meditation centre and a nearby community where we organized meditation retreats, built our own houses, grew organic food and delivered our own babies. I loved the bush but had no inkling of ecology and so, when some neighbors got on the stage between bands and appealed for help to protect the Terania Creek rainforest from logging, it was only neighborliness that inspired me to show up. Years later we realized that the direct action at Terania Creek was the first time in the world that people took direct action in defense of a rainforest.

JOHN SEED

I was about five years old. My grandfather had died and one day after the funeral I watched as my grandmother made offerings to him at the altar. I asked to be able to light a stick of incense for him and my mother tried to deny me the privilege. I was angry that I couldn't do this one last thing for my oji-isan *and made a huge fuss until my grandmother vetoed my mom. In all the confusion of a five-year-old mind, I could still feel the relationship between what I want (desire) and what I could do (power). And I am, to this day, very stubborn and fierce about it.*

ANAAR

My greatest desire has always been to be a writer, and I felt that courting from the age of four. Like many children, I folded paper in half and wrote a book with stick figures and captions, but I'm most intrigued by the back page, where I synopsized the book—"Baby Bobby is a book about a baby"— and then wrote: "The auhtor [sic] is Tananarive Due." I didn't know how to spell the word "author," but I knew what one was, and I was declaring my desire early.

TANANARIVE DUE

Chapter 1

KNOW YOUR DESIRE

There are many ways to approach the power To Know. We study books. We study ourselves. We study the world. We take the time to assimilate our study and to allow the information to deepen into knowledge. Knowledge is the result of taking in information and making it our own. Given enough time and a good dose of passionate engagement, knowledge can expand further, becoming wisdom. This requires all of our powers of rationality, coupled with our growing ability to know in the heart and in the belly. Engaging the power To Know is helped by the perspective of the eagle, the first part of the Sphinx.

When we speak of knowing our desire, however, we often need to begin from a place that feels a lot like faith. Some clearly feel desire, even if they can't pinpoint exactly what form it takes. Others have some vague longing just to *have* a desire. I'm here to tell you, that is also desire.

Desire connects us to ourselves and to the flow of life.

The magical dictum To Know has many facets and stages. Each person reading these words is likely at a different stage in his or her relationship with the manifestation of both knowledge and desire. Before coming to a place of knowledge, we first need information, experience, and some level of integration. Knowledge does not, therefore, spring full blown from the mind. It requires a combination of intellect, emotion, and, on even deeper levels, the intuition brought forth from the body. We cannot think our way to desire, but our thoughts can help us gather information, assess it, give it context, and name it. As we have seen in fairy tales throughout time, naming is a powerful activity.

In this section, we will practice approaching knowledge through thought, sense, and emotion. We will bring it to our bodies. Through all these means, we shall seek to know.

LEARNING TO LISTEN; LISTENING TO LEARN

How can we open to knowledge of self and the power to know our desire? By learning to listen more deeply.

Most of our lives are crowded with the bustle of jobs, family, advertising, television, shopping, cleaning, and cooking, making it quite difficult to hear anything but the clamor. We are also riddled with a constant barrage of thoughts and emotional states, sometimes brought about by our very wish to know what it is we are supposed to be doing! All of this makes deeper knowing feel impossible. How can we hear the voice within that is deeper than our day-to-day concerns?

By listening.

By opening to listening, we open to the whispering of the sacred to our souls. We say to ourselves and to the cosmos: "I seek the power To Know, and in seeking this knowledge, I begin here, within myself."

When I do soul readings for clients, I often say: "Take a breath. Let's go a layer deeper . . ." This helps both of us to open again, to listen again, and to have greater access to the information that wants to flow through. We start off by tuning in and listening. In the rush of vision and voice, however, we often need to pause and drop into an even more acute place of hearing, sensing, and seeing. I'd like to do that with this topic now. Let's drop a layer deeper in examining our relationship to listening. We'll go ever deeper, layer by layer, as this book and our practice progress, particularly in the segment "To Keep Silence," but let us try for a bit here.

Why do we run so hard from listening? Listening is the best way to get clear information that can be digested into knowledge. Yet many of us still decide we don't need to show up for this portion of our work. We would rather be busy, or pile on excuses, or numb ourselves—anything rather than slow down enough to take in what is really present. There are many reasons for this, of course. One is that some of us fear what will be revealed if we drop deep enough for emotional states to rise. Others fear that they will have to change their systems of blame and responsibility. Still others fear that everything will fall apart if they stop taking care of everything for the time it takes to slow down and just be with themselves. Take a few moments right now to breathe, find your center, and ask yourself if any of the above scenarios, or any others, apply to your situation.

Here's a simple example from my own life. I used to finish other people's sentences chronically. It has become a great practice of mine over many years not to do so. I particularly like to practice with Tony, who has a severe stutter.[9] He comes into the soup kitchen where I volunteer, and it is great to slow down further

---

9. With the exceptions of our Wise Council and a few well-known individuals, all names throughout this book have been changed in order to protect the privacy of people whose stories I tell.

inside and wait while he gets his words out. This sort of practice helps me learn more, and teaches me not to *assume* that I know what he means. It allows for greater discovery.

On the occasions when I do finish someone else's sentence, I'm drawn up for a moment by the realization that I've lapsed out of presence and into assumption. This happens sometimes with one of my partners—another highly verbal type. Intellectual exploration and even sparring are a big part of our relationship, but sometimes the mercurial nature of speech and thought gets in the way of deeper listening. Sometimes he finishes my sentences and I become annoyed because, no, that was not what I was going to say at all. Moreover, it interrupts the flow and measure of my thoughts. Sometimes I do the same with him. And then I attempt to return to my practice.

A companion to this practice of mine is to ask: "What do you mean?" This question advances inquiry, discovery, and learning. When I was young, I just assumed that I knew what someone else meant. My brain was so clever—of course I had it figured out! Or I felt embarrassed to let on that I might not know, so I just assumed that I knew enough. This meant that I was not able to learn as much as I might otherwise have done. My unwillingness to ask questions meant that I was impeding my own growth and development.

Slowing down enough to listen or ask questions helps me to learn. It also creates space for a richer relationship with the world around me—with myself, with Nature, and with the humans with whom I interact. I listen to the Gods, too. Sometimes they have insights I never would have come up with on my own. This is true of the collective mind as well. Collectively, we remember things we may have forgotten as individuals, or we may bring back nuggets of wisdom from our trips to the river.

Some people have a problem opposite to my own: they ask too many questions because they are forever second-guessing themselves. There is no trust that rises from their bellies toward their hearts and minds that says: "Yes! This!" They are not willing to risk making a bald statement or taking a stand for fear of being wrong. This is another form of non-presence and not listening. When we don't listen well enough to ourselves or our deeper connections, we don't interact from a place of strength. This tendency, masquerading as inquiry and learning, can actually keep us from learning the big things that are only taught when we risk failure.

When I allow myself to listen well enough with my whole being, to be present with the vibration of the earth and the person or task in front of me, when I allow time and space to enter my awareness, I don't have to race to finish the unknown. I can hear the voice of someone else supplying words I might never have come to on my own. Then I can speak with greater authority and confidence. When we open to deeper states of learning—those not run by avoidance, hubris, or fear—we can better know ourselves and better teach each other.

When we allow the powers of air, thought, and speech to flow around and settle within us—when we are not racing to finish the sentences written by the universe—we allow for a deeper relationship with self and the whole cosmos in the process. What facets of desire are lost to us because we assume our story is already written, or that we know all the answers? Or conversely, what facets are lost because we think we can never know—that our ideas and dreams can never come into reality?

I cannot stress enough how important listening practice has been in my life. Yes, it has enabled me to be a better friend, a better lover, a better teacher. But it has also helped me be a better companion to myself, to holy Nature, and to the Limitless Divine.

Two Stories about Listening

Rachel, who was taking an online class with me, said this:

> I didn't even know until this week that listening could also mean listening to yourself or listening to nature. I thought it meant understanding, agreeing with, and obeying someone else's words. I have had some fun experiences listening to others this week without effacing myself.

True listening is never self-effacement. We bring the whole self to the process, rather than denying self. When we truly listen, we aren't just waiting for someone else to decide something so we can get on with things, or so we don't have to decide for ourselves. We aren't giving away our own powers to be seen and heard. When we listen, first we listen to the parts of ourselves that are curious, in avoidance, afraid, angry, or proud. Then we can take a breath and sink, allowing those parts some space alongside the spaciousness of not knowing.

Sam wrote:

> I never really considered listening as a solution to knowledge and learning my true desire. Up to now, I've always figured that these are questions to be worked out by my intellect.

Body, mind, emotion, and spirit all engage in listening. All of them contribute to the power To Know. The process of self-knowledge is a long one; so is the process of knowing the world. But the process, should we choose to engage it, is well worth it. It doesn't mean working things out in our heads. Though cognition is a factor, we need more input than that To Know. We need to take data, translate that into information, and then allow that to deepen into knowledge. That takes a certain amount of stillness, and a willingness to be open.

If you think you do not know your desire, consider how deeply you are listening, and with what parts of yourself. The mind is your ally, but cannot do this work on its own. Listen to your heart. Your gut. Your likes and dislikes. The voices of your friends. Listen to the wind and stars.

THE QUIET INSIDE

When teaching psychic skills, I always start classes with getting quiet inside, because there is no way to access intuition and psychic information with any consistency if we do not make space for it. I return to this throughout the sessions, because of course, as our personalities become activated, we forget to remain anchored. We start to reach instead of opening.

Reaching is the way the over-culture teaches us to "fix" things. We are taught to fix problems starting from the outside and working in, rather than working from the inside out. It is no wonder that there is little change of substance on a cultural level. To know ourselves first requires the recognition that we do not know. That is where we begin. So how do we come to know? We begin by learning to listen, and then by making space.

We need to get clear inside. Filling up more in our exhaustion by surfing the Internet or watching television does not help. I'm not saying that either of these is intrinsically wrong. I am saying, however, that when we need space and time and rest, habits of distraction serve only to fill us up more thoroughly with all the things we don't need.

What would our lives be like if we chose to take ten minutes to sit quietly and watch the birds in the morning, or to sit in front of a candle in the evening? What would our lives be like if we took time to focus only on sinking more deeply into ourselves and, from that deeper place, opening out and listening with our whole Being?

I can guarantee that, over time, our lives would change. Deeply listening makes it possible to get a glimmering of knowledge about what our desire is and where it wishes to lead. Without this listening, confusion reigns. We cannot know if there is no *space* made for knowing. Data is not the same as information, which is not the same as knowledge and these days, we have more information available to us than we can ever hope to assimilate. The only way out—is in.

DESIRE AND THOUGHT

Our life is what our thoughts make it.

MARCUS AURELIUS

In discerning desire, it is important to know the workings of the mind. Systems of magic and meditation both ask us to learn to still our minds. What do they mean by this? In my experience, it means to expand the mind and deepen our presence, stretching the spaces between our thoughts so that energy and a stronger sense of self, Nature, and the cosmos can enter. We cannot know our place in the world nor discern our deep desires if our minds are rapidly flitting from one thing to another or bulldozing through our lives taking hold of every emotion. To know desire, begin with self-knowledge.

We can do practices to help us find that spaciousness of mind at the same time that we are training our habitual thoughts toward that which we desire. There are many books written on this subject, and my previous two go into various techniques for building presence of self and stillness of mind and heart (see *Evolutionary Witchcraft* and *Kissing the Limitless*). Presence and stillness are important, and I suggest seeking out various techniques to help with this. What I wish to speak to now is the shifting of your habitual thought.

Whether or not you have uncovered what feels like a deep, abiding desire, you must be aware of desire cooking within you, or you would not even be interested in this subject. We begin where we are, not where we wish to be, or where our friends or family wish us to be. What circumstance or inner voice caused you to pick up this book at this time? Some desire, known or unknown, led you to it. To court this desire, you must train yourself *toward* this desire.

A writer writes. A painter paints. A dancer dances. A magician works her magic. What do you do? Whatever it is, it forms your life. To what do you return? What do you uncover and unfold? When we do what we set out to do, we become these things. Once ignited, we have the power to shape ourselves, our lives, and our landscapes. Those of us who live in privilege relative to other people on the planet may have a greater opportunity for this, but everyone has a choice—at least in the small things, if not in the large ones.[10] Do you notice these choices, or do you simply tell the story that outside influence runs your thoughts, emotions, and physical reality?

---

10. I often use the Greek philosopher Epictetus as an example of a person who, though born a slave, freed himself inside and left a lasting legacy.

We can start with something that is both simple and quite difficult—even dangerous, in a liberating way. Each time we find ourselves churning out one of our typical stories, or catch our minds spinning in one direction or another, we can pause for a moment and say: "I desire to know my mind. I desire to know myself. I desire to live a life of clarity and purpose." This does two things: it momentarily interrupts the habit, and it begins training us into a new pattern—a new habit that is more helpful to the seeding and eventual flowering of desire.

Our thoughts affect our direction. Just as when you turn your head to look left your bicycle goes that way, so do your thoughts and emotions steer you. What do you want to guide you? Resentment? Fear? Petty competition? Lack of worth? These sorts of things steer us one way or another, but not toward inner greatness—not toward lives that will likely inspire others or give us deep satisfaction. If we wish to garden, we must train our thoughts toward gardening. Make space in your mind for desire, and destiny will alter its course.

It is difficult to create the lives we want if we cannot even catch a glimpse of them. Opening space in our thoughts helps, simply because, all of a sudden, our imaginations have room to work! If I look at the gifts or blessings I already have (whether they feel meager or great), I train myself to see the world as a place where I get gifts and blessings. Also, I enable myself to notice more often the small kindnesses offered or the little things that may be going right.

In writing about this, I'm not trying to discount real pain, terrible suffering, or bald injustice. All of these exist, and many of us live with the consequences of these in our lives. But until we can open up our sense of anger or victimization and see the ways in which we can also be heroes, it will be that much more difficult to change our own lives, let alone the lives of those around us. I have turned my life around and have seen others do the same, sometimes while facing intense hardships. Desire was persistent and helped to guide me and these others toward a more integrated life. As more integrated beings, we are now better able to help others and give back in gratitude.

How do you start? I know how I started. I shifted the way I spoke to myself internally. This trained my thoughts, and training my thoughts shifted my actions, which served to change my life. It was not the only factor in the equation, but without this step, I do not think I would be where I am today. I feel grateful for the power of the mind and its ability to help us toward great change.

Soul Support

Slow down your breathing. Try to listen to the pulse of the blood in your body. Remember that there is stillness inside you, deep in your core, near the bowl of your pelvis. As your attention sinks into that space, imagine the energy around your skin opening, expanding, and relaxing.

Imagine your life as it is. What do you spend most of your time doing? Do you get a sense of satisfaction from this activity? Notice any physical, mental, or emotional responses to this image of your life. Is there a thought you want to introduce into your life that will help you toward change? Or a thought you want to interrupt? Breathe life into the space those thoughts occupy.

Now remember one beautiful, kind, or inspiring thing that happened yesterday. Focus on that beauty, kindness, or inspiration. Let the feeling of it suffuse you. Remember that there is always some small thing that is a gift in life. Give thanks.

Can you do this every day?

SELF-AWARENESS

Self-awareness is the antidote to self-consciousness. Becoming self-aware is the key to success. It is the key to opening our lives to our destiny, our souls' work, and what we truly love. The work of our hands and minds also becomes the work of our hearts. The more we live from the place of self-awareness, the less we ratchet between self-absorption and its cousin, self-consciousness. We are present with our full selves and therefore have no need to be self-referencing in every moment. When you are self-aware, you are more decisive; when you are self-aware, you have access to greater generosity. Everyone gains.

Start—here, now—by finding your center. Start—here, now—by sitting in self-observation, getting to know your patterns, and spending time with yourself in ways that form actual intimacy rather than assumptions about who you are based upon your old stories, wounds, or triumphs. Self-observation is not psychologizing—my word for telling stories about what we think we are. It is learning to be present with who we actually are, in all our parts.

True self-awareness is the antithesis of the solipsism that posits that nothing outside of us actually exists. When we have done a measure of work toward knowing ourselves, we generate energy from our essence—our Being—and live, move, talk, and laugh from that. Everything around us begins to fall into place, because we are living a truly authentic life.

Let's examine that word, "authentic." Often, when I hear people use it, I cringe. Why? Because it gets bandied about with little clarity and can mean whatever an individual wants it to mean in the moment. It can mean: "I need to show you my vulnerable underbelly so you see how sensitive I truly am." Or it can mean: "I can express my anger and irritation because that is how I really feel right now." In these cases, the word "authentic" comes to mean: "I am acting out whatever emotion feels most present to me in the moment." In other cases, it means: "I wear these clothes, listen to this music, hold that opinion, and you can't change me."

None of these uses of the word "authentic" show me that these individuals have done the hard work of sitting with themselves on a daily basis—observing their own thoughts and emotions as they go, watching their responses to outside stimuli, gauging action or reaction over time, facing demons and shadows and desires, coming to know what they truly want. They show me individuals who may be trapped in dreams of their own making—dreams that include a skewed concept of authenticity. When used in these cases, the phrase "authentic self" often becomes a stand-in for true authenticity and a pointer toward solipsism or self-consciousness. Or, on the flip side, unconsciousness—e.g., "I don't know why you are so upset about my behavior at last night's party. I was just being myself." But which self?

To be truly authentic—to know ourselves—we need to be in touch with as many of our parts as we are able. We need to have examined the ways in which they work with and against one another. Most of all, we need to have contact with the part that is connected both to our smallest inner spaces and to the vast reaches outside of our particular selves. This part is often known as genius, or God Soul, or Holy Guardian Angel. This is holistic, and holism is what I think people are trying to point to when using the word "authentic." Used in this way, the word can mean: "This is truly who I am, all of me, animal, human, and divine. This is me, connected to the source, to my core, whether in the midst of grief, joy, anger, or quietude. There is something inside of me that simply Is."

What is your relationship to your deepest wisdom and highest source of connection? How often are you attending to these parts?

THE FEELING OF DESIRE

When we discuss knowledge, we usually do so in the context of the mind. However, it has been my experience that, until something enters my body and allows my emotions to engage, I don't truly learn, and I don't actually *know*.

The sequence of events will be different for each person, depending on whether or not the individual tends to be intellectually based, emotionally based, or kinesthetically based. Since I tend to prefer the mind, engaging my body always gives me better access to my emotions, and once all three are working together at even a basic level, I can take information in deeply and process it into knowledge. Those who are more emotionally based may need to engage the mind. Those who are body-based may need to access either mind or emotions along with the physical in order to come to a more complete understanding.

This is why the magical power To Know can feel so tricky. By what means do we know? What does knowing actually entail? While the magical power To Dare clearly encompasses emotions, we are well served to see how all parts of the self can be involved in all of the Four Powers. Each pass through knowing, daring, willing, and silence brings more of you to the task of courting desire. Do not despair if you don't know how to approach desire yet; I have faith that you will.

Meredith, a talented psychic, had almost completely shut down. She was blocked from recognizing the powerful spiritual guidance to which she had access. At about our second or third session, I mentioned that there was a very bright light I sensed just behind her, and that it was there to help her. She responded with fear. We worked through that, step-by-step. She collapsed quite easily back into not knowing, because that had become her default state. Her body responded with severe neck and back pain. However, her talent just pushed harder. When she finally opened to it, great changes in her presence and ability opened up as well. She became better able to relax the grip her emotions had on her body and to let the energy and information move through her.

We had to speak to the parts of Meredith that were afraid, that didn't know what would happen if things started to change too much, too quickly. Those parts were right to try to protect her way of life—they had established safeguards long ago to keep things relatively happy and stable—but that role was no longer helpful. It was time for her to embrace herself fully in the good life she had built. Over time, we found other ways for these parts to act as guardians. Meanwhile, her intuition came back at full power and became useful in running her business.

Starling came to a workshop. During the course of the weekend, she kept coming back to a wish for partnership. Obviously, she was in pain. Yet also clearly, she had not done much about this other than to feel it and to fantasize about it. She had cursorily explored a couple of Internet dating sites, but nothing quite panned out. It became very clear to me that she had never fully committed to loving herself first. She had become trapped in a story of being alone and unloved, and of seeking love forever. She was enamored of this story, and it came to define her. Rather than getting out and enjoying the world, she stayed home and played interactive games on her computer for hours at a time. Rather than choosing clothing that made her feel attractive, she dressed as a person who was always at home alone—baggy jeans, a loose flannel shirt, comfortable clogs.

There is nothing wrong with feeling comfortable. As a person ill at ease in her own skin, however, Starling wore her clothing like a mask, rather than as a reflection that she truly enjoyed a comfortable life. Comfort inside is reflected outside. Moreover, the discomfort she carried spilled over into other areas of her life. She chose not to like her job and resisted it, despite the fact that people thought she was good at it. It was not what she felt she wanted, but she wasn't sure how to apply herself to work she might like more. All of her spare energy was spent on longing for a thing that seemed unattainable. She desired to be seen, yet hid from the world, and even from her own heart.

What she wanted was something nebulous, defined in her mind as a lover. My sense was that what she desired on a deeper level was clear and full connection. That had to begin with herself. No one and nothing else could give that to her. Her longing—an overriding, sometimes overwhelming, want that can feel like the aching of need—had obscured her desire. After trying several approaches to make connection with some part of her that could see or feel beyond the tale of "I really want a lover," I finally asked the question: "How attached are you to your stories?" I could feel a pausing in her whole being as the question penetrated. The whole room took a breath as the energy changed. The question was, of course, directed toward us all.

MAKE MAGIC OF YOUR LIFE

In order for us to wake up—to take a risk and dive a few layers deeper—we ultimately have to confront our stories. Our energy, thoughts, and emotions get bound up in these tales we all tell, sometimes for years. All of a sudden, we may wake up one day—fifty-five years old and lonely, or twenty-seven and confused—wondering how in the world we got there. What has impeded our connection to our deeper desire? Sometimes we need to excavate, layer by layer. We have to be willing to begin to tell a different story—a more nuanced story with different characters, more substance, and brighter light. We have to be willing to change.

There is a chance for these women, just as there is a chance for all of us. Every moment holds another opportunity. The more willing you become to open up to a fresh perspective, the closer you are to touching your desire. Something deep inside you knows what you desire, whether you can admit to it or not. By letting your emotions point you toward your deeper truth, this knowing part can become your guide.

Soul Support

Take a breath with me. Feel the place in you where tears reside. Feel the place where anger constricts you. Now feel the place in you that is filled with longing. What is that longing? What part of you longs? What does it want? Home? Hope? Love? Acquisition? Destruction?

Can you feel desire in your body? Can you sense the way your stories try to block this feeling? What in you can shift, even the smallest amount, to allow a deeper knowledge to surface?

Breathe more deeply, imagining the air can fill your whole body. Let your next exhalation "push" the edges of your energy out farther, making more space for desire to dwell. What inside you will open, soften—or strengthen—and change?

LIGHTING THE FIRE

For the correct analogy for the mind is not a vessel that needs filling, but wood that needs igniting.

PLUTARCH

What lights a fire in the mind? That fire, well tended, can ignite an entire life. It illuminates passion, and passion causes us to act from a place of rooted love. By love, I mean the deep, powerful, earthshaking force that connects us to All. I mean the subtle song that insinuates itself into our hearts and will not leave. By love, I mean the kindling of something that feels so true that it lights up the world.

The Egyptian God Osiris was dismembered out of jealousy, and joined together again by the love of Isis. Jesus was derided and eventually killed. Sufi mystic Mansur Hallaj was martyred for speaking his connection to the ultimate truth, his heart on fire for his beloved—God. Hindu poet Mirabai wandered the streets consumed with the face and song of Krishna. People thought she was crazy, and her family tried to poison her. Still, she followed her desire, composing poems of ecstasy. Activist Martin Luther King, Jr. desired freedom and justice for the oppressed. Journalist Ida B. Wells refused to be trapped by gender, race, location, or attitude. Her desire was to live fully, to speak out, and to work for justice. These beings—whether we consider them divine or human, hero or ordinary person—were not dissuaded from their core, no matter what hardships arose. They all knew their calling, enacted their will, and were filled with the fires of desire.

When we can open ourselves to what is unknown, to what is new and possible, the pull of desire becomes stronger, and our course gains clarity. In subsequent chapters, we will look at resistance. For now, I encourage you to slow down your breathing and take in deeper breaths than you might usually. Allow the air to move through you, fanning the flame in your mind and opening places that feel constricted. Imagine that, where breath flows, a fire is ignited and desire follows.

I feel grateful for all the things that continuously light the fire in my mind, illuminating my soul. Do you? Breathe that in.

Action

1. Listening requires a commitment to clearing. Clearing your space is a good start. Clean the kitchen or sweep the floor. Don't wait until everything is perfect to settle in; do what you can, bit by bit. Then you can access whatever practices you have to quiet your mind and heart—even temporarily. Even if, at first, you only open up thirty seconds of stillness within the ten minutes in which you make your attempt, that is thirty seconds you did not have access to before. And who knows? Tomorrow it may increase to one minute, and then five, then back to thirty seconds once again. All of this practice, including periods that feel like setbacks, serves to train your psyche toward the knowledge that will lead you to desire.

2. When you mask yourself with stories, you lose sight of your desire. You may be filled with longing, but your life is not on course. What stories are you telling about your life right now? Can you reach beneath that story to something deeper? Can you touch the beating heart of desire, even for one moment? Engage self-knowledge on a physical and emotional level. Begin to track your stories. Make a list of them. Feel what emotions are invested in these tales. Notice how they affect your posture and bodily tension, the clothes you wear, or the food you eat.

3. How do your body and emotions react to knowledge? What can you learn from these responses?

CHAPTER 2

NEEDS, WANTS, AND DESIRES

In exploring the magical power To Know, it helps to distinguish between wants, needs, and desires, as well as between fantasy and desire. These are easy to confuse, partially because of the way English is used, and also because we aren't trained toward discernment. When it comes to looking at ourselves, we can tend toward avoidance, self-aggrandizement, or self-deprecation. How can we know ourselves under these conditions, let alone figure out whether we want something or need it?

Wanting something is fine. Needing something is also fine. We can either want or need something on many different levels. There are physical wants and needs. Emotional and mental wants and needs. Spiritual wants and needs. There are also ways in which we can substitute the words for one another, but this can cause confusion when we attempt to discern what is really going on. And this confusion is compounded by inserting the word "desire" into the equation.

Desire is a driving force, an abiding wish, a deep well, a guiding light, a burning fire. Want is a component of desire, but it is not the whole of it. When trying to discern your desires, it is a good idea to begin watching your language around want and need.

When we actually need something, are we able to ask for it? "I feel a need for more verbal support around this project." Do we allow ourselves to say "I *want* that new shirt" when we have plenty of serviceable shirts at home, but this particular shirt strikes our fancy? Sometimes, we both downplay and inflate our wants by saying instead: "I *need* this shirt!" But this leads us to believe that it is not okay to want something. It can also make it more difficult to express a real need when one comes up.

Saying we need something when we really want it, and vice versa, confuses our emotions and makes it more difficult to communicate clearly to ourselves what is actually going on internally. This, of course, compounds the difficulty in communicating wants and needs to other people and to the cosmos.

Wants come and go. Even needs can ebb and flow over time. Desire crops up again and again. It is the thing to which we always return—the itch that doesn't quite get scratched. Desire contains want, but not only want; it also includes a need that arises from heart and soul. We feel this need on a more cosmic level than the need for food and on a deeper level than a need for physical exercise.

The followers of philosopher G. I. Gurdjieff sometimes speak of "the Wish"—a profound sense of desire that suffuses our whole being, causing us to want to work hard enough that we will do almost anything to pursue it—risking physical challenge and emotional discomfort, and figuring out how to arrange time in desire's favor. The "Wish," in this case, is usually for self-knowledge, or human wholeness. It is a beautiful illustration of what I mean by desire, though desire may look a bit more prosaic and varied than the quest for self-knowledge. But really, we are speaking of similar things.

Any process toward mastery requires some work on self-knowledge, although (clever beings that we are) we can try to run from that in myriad ways! Those with a deep desire to express themselves through the power of dance are also seeking a way to put their souls together. People who know they want to put great puzzles together and help others do the same may end up running a nonprofit that finds ways to get food from local farms to soup kitchens and family shelters. Or they may end up in a school for mechanical engineering.

Acquiring even the most rudimentary knowledge of a wish or a desire is the first step toward being able to move toward acts of will. Fantasy is nice for a time, but leads us nowhere in the long run—unless want and need come together, shifting what began as a fantasy into a strong and motivating desire.

OBSESSION OR DESIRE?

Question: Why do we desire things that are bad for us? Is that truly "desire" or something else masquerading as desire?

Since I like to think of desire as the place where want meets need, I do not call those things that are bad for us desires. I call them obsessions, fantasies, or impulses.

Desire runs deep; want runs shallow, even when it feels as if we may die if we don't get what we want. Want that feels like that is often simple obsession, which becomes another mask when looking at what is actually good for our bodies and souls. As a matter of fact, the coupling of body with emotion can create some perfect examples of wants turned toward obsession.

When I was around nineteen, I had not yet found a way to be happy in my life, nor had I yet done the amount of work necessary to gain right relationship with my body. I recall one evening when I was reading in bed and thinking obsessively about ice cream, of which there was none in my shared household. I didn't really have money to spare on ice cream, as I barely made enough to pay rent and buy basic food. But the pull toward ice cream was so strong that I remember getting out of bed, getting dressed, and walking to the store for a pint of the rich creamy stuff. I had an emotional need that I was trying to fill via this physical want. Neither was desire. Ice cream was not what I really needed; I just became obsessed with it that evening because I could not even articulate what my actual needs or wants were, let alone go about fulfilling them.

If we extrapolate from this prosaic example, we can see larger patterns that turn into obsessions, sometimes leading to marriages, trips around the world, or engagements with projects that end up eating our lives, driving us in unhealthy ways toward narrower and narrower corridors of being, and sometimes leading to explosion or collapse. Some escape this by moving in the opposite direction toward fantasy and never getting much of anything done, unhappily daydreaming their lives away. Neither obsession nor fantasy is true desire. Both of them instead become avoidance of desire, a way to sidestep doing the work necessary to uncover ourselves over time in order to reveal what wants, needs, and desires we may actually have.

Moving toward desire requires a willingness to take risks. There are many steps in this process and, whether foolhardy or shy, we can all look at what sorts of risks feel both frightening and compelling to our souls. That which scares yet still attracts often points toward the road of desire.

Another way to tell if something is bad for us is to ask how it is affecting the rest of our lives. Does it feed us or drain us? Does it support healthy relationships or drive them away? What helps us be at our best and causes us to feel confident and centered? What throws us off center or causes us to feel badly about ourselves or our lives? In answering these questions, we begin to notice the active effects our choices have on our lives. This information enables us to make choices geared toward our overall health and happiness. It also shows us when and how we may be blaming outside forces or people for situations we can adjust ourselves, or how we may be taking on more than our fair share of responsibility. Adjusting your life as much as you can in any given circumstance increases your awareness, your power, and your confidence. And confidence supports your magic.

Desire should fill us with energy, with spark, with fire, with the wish to move forward. Yet desire should not consume us, eating our life energy, leaving us a husk. It should spur us toward learning, practice, and other applications of will. It may enable us to dare—to take risks we did not know we could even chance. It should not drive us until we become ill, or abandon our loved ones, or stay up all night every night. In the long run, obsession eats our life energy, while desire and passion feed it. Passion is full engagement with life, and desire is a goad toward passion. Without desire, there is no entry into passion; without passion, there is scant fuel for engagement. Without engagement, there is less and less presence. Without presence, it is harder to feel whole—not the wholeness of being finished, of perfection, but the wholeness of what Jen Louden calls "enoughness," a sense that your soul and heart have met this moment and that this moment can meet the rest of your life.

Obsession leads to behavior that can look very much like addiction and can end up running our lives. Desire and passion, on the other hand, are energies that enable us to develop still more will, more autonomy, and more skill at driving our lives. The idea of desiring—knowing that this is something we want—leads us into will, into building support for the knowing. And this leads us into risk, into daring to push a little farther than we thought we could. And this, in turn, leads us toward the silence of integration and gestation, which leads to still deeper knowledge and on toward mastery.

ORDINARY BRILLIANCE

Question: What can we do when we feel frustrated that we cannot seem to touch the core idea of what our deepest desires really are? When we have feelings around them, but not the ability to articulate them? When we recognize that we must somehow be standing in our own way?

Not all brilliance is extraordinary. Some of us get the bolt out of the blue, the crystalline perfect answer, the guidance we have been waiting for. Others lead lives of ordinary brilliance, driven by small feelings, by intuition, and by a subtle unfolding—moment by moment, day by day. Either way, our work is the same. We show up. We take the next step. We commit to becoming ourselves.

Yes, we sometimes stand in our own way, but not being able to articulate our deepest desires fully is not necessarily a sign of this. Our response to what we may perceive as a lack of brilliance can, however, become a new way to stand in our own way, to slow ourselves down, to let doubt creep into our lives. If we can allow the feelings we have—whether ordinary or extraordinary—to be the first step toward knowing desire, we can act accordingly. We can follow those feelings and keep listening for the answer to the question: "What is my work right now?" By showing up on a daily basis and learning to listen, little by little, we learn to trust the guidance of our inner voices.

We often make the mistake of thinking that our desires need to be something large, showy, or grand. For some of us, this may be the case; but for most of us, this is not so. For many, following their desire feels ordinary, even when it doesn't look that way to the outside. Even for a rock star, following desire means practice, time spent writing music, time spent keeping fit, time on the tour bus, grinding out the miles on the road, laughing a lot or getting snippy with bandmates and managers, having a blood-sugar crash, or running on too little sleep. Ordinary time. What the rest of us see are those moments onstage, all lit up and larger than life. What the rock star sees are all the hours spent just showing up.

Your deepest desire is sometimes helped by being articulated; but at other times, it can feel hindered by being pinned down too much with words. What is best for you? Find that. I would hazard to guess from looking at my own life and the lives of clients, heroes, and friends, that most of us take that deep sense of unarticulated "something" and use that feeling as a litmus against which we test the answers to the question: "What do I want to do today?" Following that energy will lead you more deeply into knowing.

How do you find that feeling? Start now, by slowing down and breathing. Take a moment for yourself. The world will still be doing its thing when you return.

Two Stories about Brilliance

Two years ago, Andi declared that she was going to have a "year of the rock star." This meant taking herself seriously, pushing beyond the forces of inertia, and really focusing on being the best partner, the best academic, the best researcher, and the best friend she could be. She was going to shine, even when that mostly meant planning more online classes, grading papers, spending time with her love, cooking meals with friends, getting some exercise, doing the research needed for her next writing project, and making sure she presented at some conferences. On the surface, this may have looked as if she was just doing her job. She was. She also shone, successfully building a niche for herself in the shifting and often collapsing field of academia. Ordinary. Yet brilliant. That is what this sort of showing up allows you to do.

Derek Sivers says that what may seem ordinary to us is often amazing to others. He writes about being in awe of other people's creations and ideas and yet, he says: "I continue to do my work. I tell my little tales. I share my point of view. Nothing spectacular." Nothing spectacular. He's just living his life and showing up for what is next. He is also a person guided by a deep desire.

How do I know this? From the outside, Derek Sivers looks pretty darned successful in pretty much every sense of the word—in music, in business, in fun. How has he done it? By showing up to what he really wants to do on a consistent basis. He did not set out to make a wildly successful music distribution company; he just saw something he both wanted and needed for himself (my definition of desire) and followed up on it (my definition of success). When the business no longer served to excite his imagination and he found his ideas and energy had been lagging for too long, he sold it for 22 million dollars. Sivers donated most of the money to a charitable trust for musicians, keeping enough to live on and start some new projects that felt interesting to him.

I'm sure that Derek feels like an ordinary guy, just doing what comes next, deciding what to have for breakfast and when to spend time with his girlfriend. What looks to us like a clear desire that he had articulated within himself from an early age probably feels to him like showing up every day, following what seems necessary or intriguing.

RESISTANCE

Sometimes we resist inspirational stories—and with good reason. Many times, they feel manufactured, unreal, and out of our reach. At other times, we cling to our own stories and refuse to look a layer deeper. And, just as each of our stories will be different, our resistance appears in many different guises as well.

When I shared Derek Sivers' story with an online class, some of the students had trouble with it, feeling that the work I described was impossible for most people, particularly those who had physical difficulties or were struggling with unemployment or depression. That launched conversations about what success looks like for each of us and how, although our stories and backgrounds may be dissimilar, we can each figure out a way to know ourselves and our conditions better, and begin to chart the path toward our desires.

In answer to the people sharing their stories and fears in our class, I knew I needed to reveal a bit more of my own journey and how I had overcome my own resistance.

I was an intellectually precocious child who was raised in a working-class, working-poor family. I dropped out of high school and then dropped out of college. I could barely afford ramen noodles half the time. I worked a lot of strange jobs to pay my rent and suffered from chronic fatigue and illness for many years. Although I mostly healed from a motorcycle accident and then from whiplash suffered while riding in a car, I ended up with chronic pain that made it difficult to work on anything. What did I do? What many of us do, I expect. Being a bit macho, at first I pushed too hard, which only increased my symptoms. When that didn't work, I still kept trying to practice, but I also rested when I needed to. I stopped doing things I thought I should be doing and started doing things I *wanted* to do. That last was a big one, because it brought me face-to-face with my own resistance and put me on the path toward my desire.

I'm not necessarily talking about giving up my job; I'm talking about giving up work on committees that no longer fed me just because they seemed like a good idea. Or planning or even attending the huge seasonal ritual I no longer liked just because everyone put effort toward it. I'm also talking about choosing to work part-time and go into student-loan debt to finish my bachelor's degree, which eventually did mean quitting full-time work at the soup kitchen and in hospice, where I was constantly exhausted, noble work though it was.

I also found a blessed homeopath who helped with my healing, treating me for almost nothing because I had no money. That was big, because seeing a homeopath meant two things: I was trusting my intuition and asking for outside help when I couldn't afford the fees. As the years went on, more and more often I chose what called to me—even when it was hard; even when two long-term relationships crumbled because of it; even when, once again, I barely had the money to pay my rent. To get through that phase, I increased my spiritual practice and figured out how best to take care of my body so that my energy flow could match the work I wanted to do.

How do you keep showing up toward self-love? How do you face your resistance? How do you keep asking your God Soul— also known as your Holy Guardian Angel or Inner Wisdom—for help? Part of what helped me, of course, was looking at my stories. And part of what helped me was choosing to practice, to meditate, to align daily. And finally, part of what helped me was learning to listen better, to shift my response to conflict, to integrate more of my parts.

ORDINARY HEROES

We do not have to become heroes overnight. Just a step at a time, meeting each thing that comes up . . . discovering we have the strength to stare it down.

ELEANOR ROOSEVELT

Heroes are beings that are larger than life, that seem to be special, set apart, not living by the rules set by the status quo. Heroes seem to make their own rules. I believe that this is true. Heroes see what needs to be done, and respond in ways that may push them beyond what they thought possible in the moment. They do it anyway. Heroes feel what is considered acceptable by society and know they just don't fit that mold. Unlike others who also have this feeling, they act and live as they will, not worrying overmuch about censure—because, really, they cannot live any other way. These people often end up blazing trails for the more timid among us to follow. They carry bodies from burning wreckage. They discover new things. They save us, somehow, by giving us an ideal to latch on to: things do not have to be the way they seem.

I love the way the ancient Greeks wrote about heroes—as products of the joining of the human and the divine. In Greek myths, a human and a God felt lust for each other and that coupling formed something entirely new—a being with something extra, whether it be beauty, bravery, strength, or cunning.[11] (In some unfortunate cases, the lust was one-sided, often leading to

---

11. I recognize that "a God" is not a proper noun. Nonetheless, when people capitalize Yaweh as "God" yet call other deities like Hera or Thor gods and goddesses, it somehow makes those Gods and Goddesses carry less weight in the world. Therefore, I capitalize Gods and Goddesses in an attempt to convey their importance.

abuse. But that is for a different treatise.) Greek heroes were thus in a class by themselves—not quite human, not quite Gods, but a little of both.

We can choose to make ourselves heroes. We can forge our own paths, cultivate our own beauty and cunning, be more than we think we are. For within each of us, in every moment, is the possibility of the human and the divine joining, bringing heaven and earth together to form something quite new.

But this requires taking risks. And because the stories tell us so, we know that heroes are *always* taking risks! That is part of why we see them as heroic. Heroes break from the safe and comfortable life—sometimes through a series of small choices, sometimes in one grand gesture. A rupture occurs in these moments—a rupture that liberates the soul. There is really no turning back at this point without causing eternal unease and forever remembering the taste and scent of freedom.

What in you feels human? What in you feels divine, or feels the touch of the divine? Are you willing to live more like a hero, one small step at a time?

Yes, we are ordinary. Life is simply as it is, and stories of heroes seem exciting simply because excitement engages our emotions and draws us in. Storytellers take the ordinary and make it seem unusual because they have the ability to see things in a new light. They are curious about life in all its permutations. Curiosity is the antidote to boredom and to feeling stuck in a rut. What will it take to make us curious about our own lives—to look upon them with fresh eyes? First of all, it takes the wish to do so, then a commitment to try. If we are not willing to do this, we keep casting about for something new, or numbing ourselves, or failing to recognize what good is currently available to us.

The ordinary is spectacular. The toothbrush waiting for the mouth. The window ready for opening. The laughter waiting to bubble to the surface. The cleansing of our tears. Even melancholy is a blessing, for it means we are alive!

A Story about a Hero

After dinner and wine in a Los Angeles living room, I listened to some works in progress by pianist (and parent and teacher) Dana Reason. I was startled by the brilliance of both the compositions and the playing itself, as well as by the fact that Dana was willing to share uncompleted work with us. And it was good. Very good.

Following the impromptu performance, several of us discussed living as creative people. Dana spoke of the difficulties of being a blond female jazz composer while the shouts of children, banished to another area of the house, rose and fell in counterpoint. Dana has trained since she was three. She spoke of the risks she takes in experimenting with forms in the midst of which she can fly. Through all of this talk of study and composition, of challenges with sexism, of industry expectations, and of the risks inherent in shifting toward new modes of expression, two threads twined tightly around each other: remaining true to self and following desire.

Is Dana a hero? She would likely say no. Yet part of her has surely gone on a journey, faced challenges and initiations, and returned home. And that part keeps courting her desire. She may not have jumped in front of a train to save a life, but she has built a good life for herself, raised children, and made music both jarringly strange and beautiful. She didn't have to be a hero to take this journey, but she did need a certain amount of courage.

For someone like Dana, I would hazard to guess, what she desires is also her True Will, the work of her God. This leaves her little choice but to follow along in hot pursuit. But what about the rest of us who may not have tapped into that yet? How do we approach desire? How do we bravely continue to follow desire, even when huge obstacles arise? How do we have the courage to remain true to ourselves and take the risk of setting down the small cup in favor of the larger? What keeps us going? And what undermines us?

Desiring is like falling in love. Or perhaps falling in love is the kindling of desire. There is an object and a subject that seek to become one thing—like a woman at her piano making music from the mind and soul. We are overcome with desire and what then? We must decide whether to pursue or thwart desire—to relegate it to the realms of fantasy or to take the risk and move toward daring.

The people who follow desire—who feel the first rush and then heroically enact their intention around it—are the ones who create art over and over, who start humanitarian or environmental organizations, who do great things, whether in the public eye or through reaching one being at a time. One definition of desire is to follow a star—setting off on a journey with an uncertain end, risking safety for the unknown. Another is to follow the beating of your own heart's rhythm, regardless of what others may think of the song.

We all want to communicate. We all want to share. But genius always includes the element of the unexpected. Surprise and courage are at the core of innovation. Do we really want to create the same things again and again? Is comfort really all we want? I don't think so, or why would desire keep occurring at the most inconvenient moments, calling us to someplace new? Even the best map cannot tell us what we will encounter on our journey. Moreover, the best journeys may begin with a charted course, but always veer off into the unknown. We must be heroes to move forward.

Soul Support

Remember a time when you felt afraid and you didn't act, or speak, or dream. How did this feel—not only emotionally, but in your body? Did it affect the set of your shoulders? Did it cause changes in your gut? Remember. Pause. Breathe. Relax.

Remember a time when you felt afraid and you acted, spoke, or dreamt anyway. How did this feel? Let your body remember. Did you tremble or feel flush with energy? Did you stand taller or want to hide? Was it a relief? Just notice. Remember. Pause. Breathe. Relax.

Find a posture that feels well supported to you. Find a way to sit or stand that gives you a sense of feeling courageous. Adjust toward that posture. Notice. Pause. Breathe. Relax.

Can you feel the excitement of being human, in this place and time, filled with possibility? What are you waiting for? No one can activate the possible but you. You are the necessary ingredient for the magic of today. Wake up to your own self. Shut the doors of cynicism. Open to that which entices, that which calls, that which is gorgeous or horrible, that which cuts to the quick, and that which burns like fire.

What some call miracles are occurring in each second. Part of the miraculous is you.

COURTING DESIRE

We all have different ways of courting desire—and we all court it in different ways at different times. Some days, we need to listen to the sound of our own voices speaking the words we wish to hear. Some days, we need to live as though we matter. Some days, we must remember who we are. Some days, we must choose to act as though we were not afraid.

Following the course of desire is not always easy; but even when we flounder and grow weary or lose sight of our goals, something pulls us on and keeps us from complete collapse. There is still some knowing—even in the idle fantasies of escaping destiny—that we do not really want to escape. We want to stoke the inner fire that is the lamp that shows the way. Will we accept the power of our own illumination? Will we wrestle with the love present in our darkness and turn struggle to embrace? There is no light or darkness within the eternal Now. There is simply this: the great dance of unfolding.

We court desire by choosing to do so. Whether it feels elusive or strong, we can find and follow the thread that binds our hearts to desire. Sit with it at your altar. Take desire out dancing. Listen more carefully to what your soul wants and needs, knowing that, in doing so, you court not only your personal desire, but the desire your soul has for the Mystery that first divided itself for love.

We come to know desire by coming to know ourselves. When you know yourself, when you kiss desire, the whole world comes alive—and that is magic.

Action

1. Take a walk through your neighborhood as if you were showing a friend who had never visited before. What do you notice? Have a conversation with a friend or family member without assuming you know what they are going to say. What do you hear? Listen to yourself on a daily basis, open to the guidance from your heart and soul. Ask more questions. Be open to different answers.

2. List three things that you want and do not have—no matter how fantastical. List three things that you need and do not have. List three things that you want and have. List three things that you need and have. Then take a deep breath. Drop into your center, the place that rests near your pelvic bowl. Breathe in and release it with a sigh, letting the edges of your self relax. Now ask yourself: "What do I desire?"

3. Choose an "I want" from your list to work on. This needn't be a big "my destiny" desire. Rather, choose something that will help you practice getting to know your wants and desires and take the necessary steps to manifest them. Really focus on what you want. Get it as clear in your mind's eye as possible. Write it down. Practice imagining getting what you want. Then choose the next step toward manifestation.

THE RITUAL OF KNOWLEDGE

... it is necessary to KNOW what has to be done.

ELIPHAS LÉVI

This ritual is simple. Do whatever helps alert your soul that you are entering a different space and time than is ordinary for you. You may wish to sit or stand at an altar, or go to a favorite place outside. Just make sure you have twenty to thirty minutes of privacy. Have a journal and pen ready to make notes when you return. It is also a good idea to have a cup of water on hand. Drink this at the end to bring yourself fully back into the present.

Imagine you can travel to your place of power, your sacred place—the grove of your heart, the cave of your soul, the temple of your mind. Relax into your body. Take five deep breaths. Let each exhalation be another step toward your sacred place. Imagine yourself entering. What does it look like? Are there trees, animals, columns, glass, brick, desert vistas, or a night sky? Is there the scent of plants or of rain on stones? Is there incense burning, snaking upward? Do ravens call or bells ring? Just notice. This is your space.

Settle in. Open to your breath. Notice how the air feels as it moves through your nose or across your tongue. Drop into a sense of stillness at your core. Breathe. Imagine a light around your head. Imagine that the stillness at your center is a companion to this light.

Say out loud: "I ask for teaching. I call down knowledge. I would know myself. I would know desire."

Let yourself just sit and breathe. Be open to the teaching that is available here. Whether it is a flash of insight, a stirring inside you, a vision, a word, or an emotion, allow yourself to breathe with that. Sometimes the teaching is a question. We can breathe with questions, too.

After this portion of your journey feels complete for the moment, imagine that you can stand up in your sacred place. Raise your arms above your head. Draw down more light, more breath, more knowledge. With your palms up and open, slowly lower your arms toward your head.

Call down the power To Know. Draw it toward you. Feel it enter the top of your head. Breathe deeply and let the possibility of knowledge fill you.

Thank this place, this time. Bow deeply. Then, on five long breaths, come back to ordinary space and time. Take a breath from the soles of your feet to the crown of your head. Remember who you are. Blessed be the power To Know.

Take a drink of water. Write down your insights, thoughts, emotions, or visions if you wish to. Rest. Be.

INVOKING THE NEXT POWER

When we can truly say "I want," we can resolve to say "I will." Knowing what we want—small or large—enables us to take the next step, to take action. That next step is a statement of our willingness to engage, to be present, and to commit to a desire.

When actions are based on "I want," even when acting on that feels difficult, stay with it and don't tip over into "I should." "I want" allows for flexibility as well! If you want spiritual deepening, then knowing you need regular prayer and meditation becomes easier—even when it feels as if you would rather sleep for ten more minutes—because the overall "I want" doesn't go away. If you are eating well on a regular basis because you want vital health, then the occasional craving for an ice cream doesn't become a battle of "should or shouldn't"; it just becomes: "I'll eat an ice cream cone now because it sounds like fun and will taste good."

"Should" is not good enough for the heart and soul. It does not well up from inside of us, crying to be seen and heard. "Should" is grudging; it lacks passion. And it often doesn't come from inside of us at all, but is something we take on from the outside. Let yourself—right now—breathe in and say the words: "I want . . ." Then take a step toward the power To Will.

Any decision, any action, can change the world.

PART II
To Will

WE ASK THE WISE COUNCIL:

WHAT MOST HELPS YOU TO FOLLOW THE COURSE OF DESIRE?

I have a commitment to achieve my goals. I don't easily give up. I look at challenges as part of life and part of the process toward achieving anything. With that basis, it is hard for me to be shaken from a course that I have committed to after much thought, deliberation, discussion, and introspection.

MIHIR MEGHANI

Rest. Meditation. Yoga Nidra. Community of like-minded people! The other components I need to follow the course of desire are lightness, sense of humor, sex, beauty, and self-trust. Self-trust comes when I make promises to myself I can keep, when I don't override my instincts and don't turn them into a story. Self-trust leads to Sovereignty which means I am at choice and that leads me right back to following the course of desire!

JENNIFER LOUDEN

Being willing to feel deeply, stalking the shadow inside me that wants to shut down, run away, withdraw. Examining my deeply held habits, addictions, and coping mechanisms. Not getting too comfortable. Clearing the slate so I can listen to what's next. Letting go of the ways I think my life should unfold. Being willing to walk forward alone—without guides or precedence. Making it up as I go along. Vigilantly staying outside the boxes that I have created for myself or that others have created for me. Moving, drumming, singing, and deep rest.

SUZANNE STERLING

Those are the two big ones to follow: What excites me? What scares me? It's rarely a big *feeling. It's usually quite subtle, and happens every day.*

DEREK SIVERS

I usually respond to a desire to create words from experiences that can feel wordless; first to create a kind of order for myself, and then, hopefully, for others. The supernatural stories I write are metaphors for the real-life horrors and losses all of us must face.

TANANARIVE DUE

Chapter 3

WILL AS MUSCLE

The power of the will is the quantity through which we achieve, produce, carry out and maintain what we aim for and what we wish for.

Franz Bardon[12]

I like to think of will as a muscle. It supports our ability to do (or sometimes not to do!). Developing will is simple. But that doesn't mean it is easy. Developing will is helped by continuous application of setting an intention and then *trying*. The power of will resides in making active choices—being *willing* to choose morning ritual over an extra thirty minutes of sleep; being *willing* to choose taking the stairs instead of the elevator if we are physically able; being *willing* to choose study instead of television, rest instead of adding one more thing to our To Do lists. Each time we make a choice that supports our desire instead of one moment's whim or want, we strengthen our ability to make longer-lasting choices. We develop the core strength that is often named the power To

---

12. A teacher who is famous not only for his treatises on magical practice. Many of Bardon's books can be found used or have been reprinted.

Will. Will develops with the strength of the lion, the second part of the Sphinx.

We make passive choices all the time. These support old patterns and habits, and often inertia. Active choice not only builds the muscle of the will, it also strengthens our autonomy and our ability to take responsibility for our lives.

We see the power of will in athletes, entrepreneurs, activists, and artists. Something drives them, for all the world to see. That drive is different for each person. For one athlete, it may be a desire to strengthen lung capacity after quitting smoking. For another, it may be a desire to stave off bone-density loss. For yet another, it may bolster a desire to compete and win. The outcome is the same, however: all three develop will—an inner strength that keeps them going and enables them to have the power to make many more choices in life, not only the choice to go for a run.

A Story about Will

I love the story of Kara Richardson Whitely, who decided to climb mountains instead of just dreaming about it.[13] How did she do this? She followed the advice she currently dispenses: "Think big; start small." She had desire, and needed to take the next steps to move from the power To Know her desire and into the power To Will her desire. What did she do? She started walking, because that was what her body had the capacity to do at the time. Of her process, she writes: "If I had said, 'I'll climb Kilimanjaro when I lose 120 pounds,' I would have never climbed the mountain. I started on flat trails, then moved to hills. As I gained strength and

---

13. Whitely is author of *Fat Woman on the Mountain*. More information can be found at *www.fatwomanonthemountain.com*.

experience, I conquered bigger mountains. Then, I was really ready to hike Kilimanjaro."

With her vision in mind at every phase, Kara literally took one step at a time. That is how will is strengthened.

FEAR

Question: Why do we have so many desires, yet we are often not able or disciplined enough to work to fulfill them?

What stands between us and our own liberation? Usually, it is some sort of fear. Not the fear that tells us something or someone is a danger to our physical bodies or emotional well-being, but the fear that something may change us.

We often give up too easily. We worry about what other people think of us, or we push our energy in ways that set out to prove we *don't* care what they think of us. These responses are really the same. We don't comprehend that, when we fully commit to ourselves, we increase our power and our presence, and liberate ourselves to do the best work we possibly can—the work the world is calling for us to do.

The formula is simple: we do what we must and what we can. We don't tie ourselves up in constant knots about it. As I've said, though simple, this is not easy, because the knots are already there. So we train ourselves to slowly untie them, then we train ourselves to meet the influx of energy that arises when the knots are loosened. We train ourselves to grow stronger, more resilient, more faithful, more trustworthy.

For whom do we do this? For ourselves. For our own souls. At first, we may do this because a teacher suggests it, or because it helps us feel better connected to the green earth or to God Hirself. But even these are temporary props. In becoming spiritual adults, we end up doing things because we must. This feeds relationships to self, to earth, to the cosmos, and to our Gods. More than that, our souls know this: It is simply the right thing to do.

In exploring this, it is helpful to notice the tension between the part that seeks and the part that resists. I remember when I was first learning nonviolent intervention—in the field, so to speak. I had a little theory, but not much. Mostly, I watched others in action. I recall the struggle inside of me: one part of me wanted to run away, another wanted to move to help, and yet another wanted to stay very, very still. The latter parts were those most strongly trained in my childhood. I could be quickly fierce to defend another, but my own defense felt too dangerous—rightfully so, given the conditions of my birth family—and my best recourse was to be small and quiet.

In the study of nonviolent intervention, I had to stay with myself and then find the moment when, with a little push, I could move toward danger with consistency. I trained myself to run toward a fight instead of away from it. Something at my core knew that I must. This was not about heroics—at least, not in any situation I can enumerate. It was about being in relationship with the world around me and *knowing* that I must do this thing. Simple. Right.

The process of training for meditation, prayer, physical exercise, love, intimacy, creative expression, or health is all the same. We have resistance. We fear something. We avoid. We long. We want this thing. We have lists of "shoulds." We observe. We try to gather information. We make excuses. We forget. One day, however, something in us has to decide to do this thing—to change our eating habits; to sit at our altars every morning; to risk rejection in order to be more fully loved and loving; to take out the canvas and the paints; to work for justice. Something in us has to decide to run toward the fight.

Once we reach that point, we have access to more help. An energy begins to stabilize within us that allows us to take on the teaching our decision is offering. We may fail three days out of seven, but the other four days give us something that we didn't have before. We keep learning. We sense ourselves in a fresh way. Our parts learn to work together. We keep trying.

Eventually, via some mysterious process, some titration, a sea change occurs. We can't go back to living in our fear. Too much of us has awakened to be lulled back into slumber. We begin to live in an entirely different way. Because we must.

SHOWING UP

What does it take to sustain desire long term? It takes showing up every day to do the work. It takes persistence. This is also known as the power To Will.

We tend to think of desire as a sharp yearning—something filled with fire and passion, a thirst that must be quenched immediately. Desire can also show its face through sheer persistence or through an abiding wish—a continued return to the well, year after year. This kind of desire follows the water back to its source. It notices the small sparks when they come and uses them to build a sustainable fire.

Remember that want and need come together to form desire, or a strong internal wish. The want may seem to come and go, and the need may cease to gnaw so intently in your belly, but you know desire remains because something always brings you back to the *practice* of desire. The practice of desire is paying attention to all the little ways we shape our lives to support the unfolding of the desire, or to avoid it at any cost because of our fears.

A Story about Desire

I'll give you an example. One weekend, I was with a group of writers on the beautiful Oregon coast. These were all people so filled with desire that they found time to write 500–2,000 words every morning of the week, sandwiched in between walking the dog and dressing for work. They mailed out story after story and wrote novels when they were not doing that. They got published and they got rejected; but they kept on writing and mailing—and still do. Nothing stops them. They are persistent in their relationship with desire. I could sense very clearly the presence of both want and need in them when they talked about their craft. Had they made it big? Some made a decent living from writing; but others held down full-time jobs on top of their writing careers. They went to these workshops to learn how to help their careers become more vital, viable, and stable, and how to improve their craft over time. Then they went home and sat at their desks or kitchen tables and wrote some more.

Sometimes we miss desire because we are looking for the lightning bolt, and then one day we wake up and realize that we have been following the ways and means of desire all along. We've been wanting the heady rush of infatuation—the flash of extraordinary brilliance—when what we really have is love—the ordinary brilliance that comes with showing up and doing the work. Our hearts are not always pounding, but they do tap out the rhythms of our lives.

Soul Support

To what do you keep returning? Those of you who are dilettantes or wanderers, flitting from one thing to the next, can you sink deeply for a moment and find a common thread? Those of you who feel as if the fog has not lifted from the vast ocean of your desire, can you feel it there, beneath the surface of your thoughts and emotions? What keeps you seeking?

How do you shape yourself according to desire, and how does desire shape you?

COMMITMENT

Question: What is the relation between desire and Will? And how do we balance desire with being free from the desire for results?

Developing will begins with willingness, and willingness starts with some small commitment. Willingness comes when we admit—even in our imaginations—that our lives, souls, and longing are worth the risk of that commitment. One day, we grow tired of waiting for our lives to appear and we see what our lives actually *are*. And we decide: "Why wait?" Sometimes the effort toward this is quite difficult, because the inertia of self-deprecation or mile-long lists of things to do crash up against the longing of our souls. But that longing does not go away; it becomes a goad in the belly. Desire, rising, must find a way. If we do not open that way, it becomes more and more painful in its constriction.

When my students or clients begin to lose traction, stalling in old patterns of inertia, I often say: "If you don't commit to yourself, who will?" This commitment is the beginning of discipline—the act of being a disciple, of taking on the teaching of each moment, each task. The more firmly and clearly we commit, the more open we are to the teaching the cosmos offers to our souls.

Sometimes, wanting the outcome of desire to look or feel a certain way becomes a big stumbling block to willing commitment. Within us in those moments is the wish to "get it right." A friend once reminded me that the larger our attempts, the less we control the outcome. In other words, to manage the fruits of will means to limit our desires. If all we want is to cook an edible dinner, the bar is pretty low. That makes it easier to match an exact outcome with that want. These smaller things are great ways to train ourselves toward a healthy relationship with will and action. They then have an opportunity to become springboards for the things that feel big.

A Story about Commitment

I know a woman who had a big desire. After the disastrous earthquake of 2010, Marcia wanted to go to Haiti and build new homes for the displaced.[14] This desire was likely undergirded by an even larger calling of which she may not even have been conscious. There were many variables at play, and there was no way she could control them all. All she could do was what she did: fly to Haiti and do the work in front of her each day. Because she was willing to commit in this way, she was successful at fulfilling her desire.

---

14. For information about her work with Haiti Communitère, visit *http://haiti.communitere.org.*

Letting go of what perfection looks like goes a long way toward bolstering our ability to have a positive effect in the world, both large and small. We will likely have to do this step-by-step, and even call upon the next power, To Dare.

Soul Support

When you commit to yourself, you commit to desire. You commit to tasting the sweet flesh of the peach and allowing the juice to caress your skin, leaving behind a sticky imprint of the sun. When you commit to yourself, you allow for desire, for the connection to the power of life itself, to rise inside of you, cresting like a wave or the belly of the moon at the horizon.

What is upon your horizon? What do you sense tugging at your soul? What is your deep, unanswered longing? Only if you take the risk to answer, to try on your desires, can you truly know if they are deeply rooted soul-calls or phantoms your personality is throwing out in order to keep you trapped in dreamland, in the land of might-have-been or cannot-be.

Every soul is a risk-taker. Some are shy about admitting it, and others feel beaten down by circumstance. But deep inside is a kernel ready to sprout with the smallest additions of sun and rain. What makes you willing to water your own garden and see what might grow beautiful and tall, what might wither and be composted, what might need to be weeded out in order to make more space for what is to come?

PRACTICE

Practice makes more things possible than we sometimes know. Meditation offers greater presence and psychic awakening. Working with our hands brings a steadiness to life. Observing the stages of a garden through planting, mulching, weeding, and harvesting tunes us to the phases of moon and sun. Practicing music every day tunes our lives. Practicing one thing can also help us to do another better.

It can feel easy to think: "I know this already. I can set it down now and move on." But without steady application of will, intention, and time, we grow sloppy, less supple, less able to use the muscles needed to get the job done, whatever that job is. Also, older habits that we thought had been laid to rest creep forward once again, and we find our minds and emotions revisiting loops that keep us ineffective and maintaining a comfortable status quo, rather than reaching for what we thought we really wanted.

Each day is time to choose again. We can all practice something. Anything. Our practice makes things possible. And that can end up feeling perfect.

A Story about Practice

One day, I broke up a fight during my shift at the soup kitchen where I volunteer. I used to break up fights often when I worked there full-time, but I hadn't needed to do so in years. That day, however, I was the one who saw the situation escalating, quickly moving from a few harsh words toward physical confrontation. I ran toward the guest I knew best, stood in front of him, and started to talk him down. When he moved to get around me at the other man, I moved with him, blocking him with my aura and body—arms out, breathing deeply, using my voice to keep the peace. It worked. He backed off. The other man left the dining hall. The guest I was dealing with sat down. He grumbled a bit, but shook it off quickly. The other people at his table gave him some space to calm down. I later saw them all talking together in a friendly manner. People sharing a meal.

Because I maintain a daily practice of re-centering and opening my energy and attention, I was able to break up the fight. My practice was supported by the active choices of my will; and my will and intention are now supported by my practice.

ENGAGEMENT

Manifesting desire requires full engagement. When we do things halfheartedly, they never gather the momentum that brings about joy and the feelings of success. Why do we do things half-heartedly? Either we don't fully understand how these things support our larger goals, or we are afraid of making a commitment to something we fear we will fail at anyway. Either of these attitudes can keep us from our larger wishes for our lives.

In 2010–11, I chose to take on a lot: ambitious projects, workshop and conference travel two to three times a month, plus maintaining relationships and working with long-term students. Consequently, I wished to monitor my energy levels so they would remain more consistent throughout the day and chose to make two changes in my morning routine—something that can feel really difficult. In the past, however, I've found that if I don't change my morning routine, nothing else really changes. The morning sets the template—energetically and attitudinally—for the rest of the day. So I added two things to my routine that my personality would tell you I hated: yoga and eating breakfast.

At first, I had to struggle to get myself to start the simple yoga routine I set for myself, although it was nothing fancy—just a series of sun salutations before meditation. There were mornings within the first week when I just did not want to do this. I really wanted a cup of tea and then meditation. But I knew that this was part of an old pattern and, if my choice was to establish a new pattern, I had to make this change first. So every day, I downed a protein shake and dropped onto the yoga mat, even though I did not want to. The result was that, only a couple of weeks into the new routine, my body wanted the yoga and took to the practice more thoroughly—with greater engagement and for a longer period. This then set me up for prayer and meditation in ways that allowed my practice to feel refreshed.

I could feel the energy moving right away; my body awakened more quickly and even grew used to eating a light breakfast. No big deal, right? Well, it was a big deal for me, being completely against past routine. I knew I not only wanted but needed to make these changes or there was no way I would have the energy to get my work done—work that I really want to manifest.

It worked. Energetically, and therefore in my work, I started kicking ass. All it took was making a decision, showing up for that first week when I did not want to, and reminding myself of my commitment. I didn't even get the usual afternoon slump, because my body fell into a better eating pattern throughout the day as a result of the new morning routine.

We have to engage to make a change. Momentum can carry us for awhile, but the day will come when we have to choose all over again. By then, our willingness to choose wisely will have been bolstered. It becomes easier to know what we desire and to will our lives to support it.

The prosaic is where the sublime starts. If magic is the art of changing consciousness at will, what I did with my morning routine was some magic. I fully engaged, step-by-step, in the service of my larger goals. That is something all of us can do. It is part of our Divine Work.

A Story about Engagement

Here is a story to illustrate how engaging fully and making active choices help us create a world that supports not only ourselves, but the community around us.

I was invited to join a Japanese New Year's celebration that included a Taiko performance. That day, in a cold concrete rehearsal space, twenty-five people stood before drums of various sizes, ranging from big to massive. They centered themselves, and showed up with as much presence as they could. Some of them had only been playing for a few months, and yet no one winced at mistakes or broke the energy. Instead, they kept riding the great dragon of sound as it rolled out toward us, bringing us into its wake, lifting us upon its power.

After the first song, the newer people knelt on the sides as the experienced drummers played progressively more difficult pieces. The lesson for me came, not only in the amazing sound issuing from the great drums, but in watching the faces of the drummers, noticing their postures, and seeing the rootedness of their feet and the strength of their thighs and arms. When I looked at the friend who had invited me, I saw a constant stream of joy lighting up her face. Her arms moved in precise patterns while wielding the acacia sticks. Her back was straight, yet supple. She struck the drums with power, the muscles in her biceps bunching and releasing. And all the while, she smiled. This was not a performer's smile pasted on for the benefit of the audience; her face and the faces of her Taiko cohort were all lit up from the inside from sheer joy.

It was then that a litany came to me: Grace. Joy. Precision. Power. This was what each person embodied; this was the rhythm they pounded out upon the waiting drums.

People so often speak of how hard the work is—how difficult it feels to keep committing to themselves, to their projects, to their spiritual lives, and to their work in the world. They speak of a fear of loneliness, of becoming too set apart from their friends and families the farther they venture on their paths. They speak of feeling clumsy as they learn, of crashing about as they step into their power. They worry as relationships around them change in order to make space for what is being wrought.

My answer to them is encapsulated in that Taiko performance. Yes, it is hard to show up in a cold cement room in the middle of winter and learn, not only complex rhythmic patterns, but centering, presence, and the exact placement of your arms and feet both in the air and on the ground, as well as where to hit the drumhead to make a precise note. Yes, it takes time. No, at first, we don't feel graceful. Yes, we can only do this work of deep inner connection alone. Something inside us has to have this wish. In that way, all of our work is solitary. Yet there also appears around us a community of other people who are working—quietly, or with loud verve.

And after we grow used to our commitment, after we sink and open—riding the dragon of energy, following the course and the flow of the sound—joy appears. Grace appears. We grow in power. We develop the ability for precision from the sheer force of our being, in presence, in this moment. Moment after moment flows outward into life.

The work is worth it. Every small commitment, each little risk, builds toward the precise arc of an arm in space, pausing at full extension—before wheeling back around to strike the drum.

CONSOLIDATION

I would know myself in all my parts.

From a Feri tradition prayer

Setting a strong intention and following through on it require that we consolidate our energy by having as much of ourselves as possible in agreement. If there are parts of us that are not yet in agreement, it helps to have them at least be party to the discussion.

We can only run from ourselves for so long by denying certain parts of our personalities and souls. Eventually, we must consolidate all parts of our personalities if we want to move toward our desire, because the parts of ourselves that cause us discomfort often hold a lot of energy and, therefore, power. Refusing to look at anger stunts our ability to feel and speak our truth. Locking away our sense of inadequacy gives insecurity a chance to sabotage us unwittingly.

In order for the power To Know and the power To Will to work together, we must come to know as much of ourselves as possible in any moment. Recapture the energy you have wasted in hiding, dismissing, wrestling, punishing, or ignoring the parts of your soul that feel problematic. When we retrieve the energy of our souls, we can put more strength behind our will. When more of our parts are working together, our actions have more clarity of purpose. Our will becomes a force for change in our lives, and in the world.

It is hard to act upon our intentions if we are working at cross-purposes to ourselves. The simple act of consolidation—of calling ourselves home—increases our ability to say: "I will." Self-compassion is a useful tool in this process.

Soul Support

Take a breath. Find the stillness at your center. Breathe into that and exhale toward your circumference, the edge of your energy field. Begin to think of all the things you have hidden, refused, or locked away. Think of the things that scare you, excite you, or embarrass you. Imagine them just outside your field, skulking, hiding, raging. Slow your breathing down. One by one, begin to call them back into your field, using the stillness at your center as a magnet. Invite them home. Breathe them in. One by one. Feel their energy flowing toward you, surrounding you, and entering you. Let yourself expand to hold this returned flow.

Practice this for as long as you feel you can, and then for three breaths more. Then send a breath up to just above your crown to feed your connection to divinity.

Do this daily or weekly, until you feel more and more of your energy has been welcomed home.

Action

1. Every morning, notice your still center point. Imagine that this rests around two inches above your pelvic bowl. Breathe into that space. Then light a candle and gaze into the flame for five minutes. Keep breathing and re-centering during this process. This allows your strength of will and presence to grow.

2. Here's a simple writing exercise. Gather pen and paper, journal, or computer. Begin by writing the words "Desire is . . ." After three to five minutes, switch to "I desire . . ." Don't try to pin anything down at this point, just let whatever wants to flow out arise. Later you can go back, look over what you have written, and sense if something jumps out at you—something that feels particularly juicy, potent, filled with life, or even frightening. Bracket this in red and write it out on its own piece of paper. This will tattoo it on your heart, beneath your skin.

3. Later in the week, look again at this potent desire. Place it at the beginning of a fresh page and, underneath it, begin to write "I will . . ." What action will you place in the service of your desire?

Chapter 4

WILL AS SEEKING

The pathway to desire is often seen as one of longing or seeking. Desire can be the precursor to devotion, or to change. There are parts of us that seek adventure, parts that feel stuck, and parts that simply have a sense that there is more to life than we are currently living. Whether you seek art, or love, or satisfying work, or spiritual integration, if you have picked up this book, you are a seeker.

The role of the seeker is an honorable one. History tells us of many who set off to explore—the shape of quarks, the surface of the moon, the inner landscape of the human mind, the depths of the ocean floor. These stories let us know that so much is possible for human beings. There is the process of picking up the kids from school, of learning a new accounting system, or of meeting friends for drinks. But there is also a wide world out there—and within—ripe for discovery.

Sometimes cultures teach us that seekers are special and that, therefore, we cannot all be seekers—that we should be content with our lot in life and settle down with what we have. For some, this will be true. Even then, however, I want to say that we can all seek. We can seek the beauty in each moment. We can seek out the blush of the apple, or the questions of children, or the sense of connection we get when we share a smile in the grocery store or bump up against someone on the dance floor. Seeking, and the grand adventure, begins right now.

I'm quite interested in what causes people to pursue their quest against strong odds. When you have gone through times where just getting out of bed felt impossible, what motivated you? What was the thread that finally pulled you out to make a cup of tea, read some news, water your plants, or call someone?

Friends help. Steady spiritual practice helps. Things that make us laugh or cry can help. Mostly, however, I've found that curiosity is one of my strongest allies. What will happen next? What can I learn if I show up in a conference room full of people in order to take a workshop that sounds intriguing, but that may be a bust? What will happen if a teacher asks me to do something just outside my usual comfort zone? What will happen if I try this new thing?

We all find ways to be inspired and, conversely, never know when a word or gesture from us will inspire someone else to become a seeker.

A Story about Seeking

While teaching "Engaging the Warrior's Heart" at a conference, it came time to spar. We were using physical sparring as a way to practice energetically saying "No thank you" and "Not about me." Everyone had already practiced strengthening the physical and energetic center of will, and we had spoken about the importance of honoring commitments, standing in truth, and opening from strength into compassion. For the sparring session, I paired myself with Ayla, a woman in a motorized chair who could only move her head and a few fingers.[15]

As we began to work, Ayla was tentative—like most people who are unused to sparring. I asked her to throw energy at me. I defended against it with a "No thank you!" and my own energetic slide to left or right. We traded off, and I hurled energy her way. At first, it penetrated. But as she got used to the activity, she began deflecting my energy with greater and greater accuracy. She found a way to engage her will and say "No thank you!" with full force. I felt her energy responding to my own.

While it never would have crossed my mind that she could not spar with me, I also realized that Ayla could just as easily not have attended a workshop that had a strong physical component. Many people might look at Ayla and think: "She would never go to a class called 'Engaging the Warrior's Heart.'" But Ayla is a warrior every day. The fact that she came, listened, and engaged for the entire class speaks to the power of her desire and her quest.

Ayla is a true seeker. She follows desire and sets her intention toward will on a regular basis, which is likely why she picked up the sparring activity so quickly—she'd been practicing in other ways. For her to attend meetings, classes, or rituals requires huge amounts of time, energy, and resource management that would daunt many of us. Yet her desire is so strong that these challenges do not stop her. She continuously seeks out spiritual connection, education, a relationship with community, and her Gods and Goddesses. She not only shows up; she is contact person for the group, teaches classes, leads ritual, and helps keep the community going.

---

15. I have Ayla's permission to tell her story.

I don't know what Ayla's deeper purpose is, but it is clear to me that she is following a strong tugging at soul level. On top of her spiritual commitments, she teaches children in public school, makes art, and writes poetry. Her intention is strong, and she acts on it repeatedly, strengthening her will in the process. Sometimes I feel her will must be indomitable, but I know that, like the rest of us, there must be days when she is tired and doesn't want to get out of bed. The thing about Ayla that impresses me is that she consistently finds a way to connect with the cosmos and do her Divine Work in the world. She continues to seek, and she does so with mobility so limited that my brain can barely comprehend it, because my experience is so different.

Ayla is ordinary. She is also extraordinary. Those who work with her get a perspective they would otherwise not have had. They often end up inspired. Like pianist Dana Reason, Ayla is a stereotype-smashing hero and a woman on a quest. Desire bolstered by will makes more things possible than we sometimes allow ourselves to imagine.

SEEKING AS PRACTICE

Let your actions speak your will.

VNV NATION[16]

When we seek a sense of connection, we open ourselves to desire and to support for that desire. Practice honors the seeker in us and strengthens that support. For some, honoring the seeker means picking up a paintbrush every day and invoking their inner artist. For others, it means sitting at their altars in prayer, contemplation,

---

16. From the song "Resolution" on the album *Automatic*.

or meditation. For still others, it is the six-o'clock run through the neighborhood they need to gain stamina for the week ahead.

We often struggle with showing up to practice—and we will dive more deeply into our fears around that in other chapters. For now, I simply want to say this: practice is about practicing. It is called practice because it is not meant to be perfect. It is there to set a foundation of help. It is there as an offering of time and attention to ourselves. Practice can take many forms, and will vary from person to person—partially because of the vagaries of personality, but also because each of us, in our seeking, needs to practice slightly different things.

Practice makes possible. It gives the seeker who longs for water a drink from the well of silence, presence, and attention. Practice tells us: "I am committed to you." It gives us structure—support beams that rise from a foundation that is our initial commitment. Think of your time commitments as a practice, rather than as an end product. So much of our struggle comes from feeling imperfect, or from impatience with trying something new.

Bringing the seeker toward practice requires practical means. What do you seek? A deeper connection? Connection to others? To God Hirself? To Nature? To the Gods? To your soul's work? What is one basic thing that will help? Not sure yet? Experiment for one to three months at a time with one or two practices. A practice set down by another, or one that you try out yourself, or a group practice you can check in with—all of these can eventually help you build your monastery, your temple, your home. Eventually, you will find a form that takes you more deeply into the process of desire—that enables your seeker to find some measure of what it has been seeking.

We are all seekers. Even those of us with occluded, suppressed, or thwarted desires have something deep inside that seeks something more. Why else would we need to numb and distract ourselves from what we want and will? We are all following some distant star. And eventually we will all come to recognize that this star resides in our very core. From this place, we move toward action.

Soul Support

Notice that in you that seeks. Notice that in you that longs to return to yourself, your soul, your deeper life. Notice that in you that wants. Let yourself open and sink a little deeper.

Take a few moments right now to close your eyes, breathe, and listen for your longing for connection. Try to sense the answers to these questions: What in you longs for deeper connection? To what do you long to connect?

Where do you feel the answers—or the avoidance of answers—in your body? Follow that physical feeling and try to find what emotion lives inside it. Ask it questions and find out what that feeling needs. Feed it cookies. Stretch. Go for a run. Mostly, take in a deep breath and imagine the edges of your skin opening and relaxing as you exhale.

What do you seek in your life? Presence? Attention? Awareness? A feeling of centeredness? A return to a touchstone? Greater connection to your path? A clearer sense of self? Self-love and self-care?

PERSISTENCE

Have you ever felt like giving up? I get notes from people saying they just can't try—that trying is for the privileged, or the healthy, or the young. They don't have the money, the joint mobility, the stamina, or the time.

I feel sympathetic to these notes and to the pain and tears in the eyes of the people who tell me their stories in person. There is much in the world by which we can feel overwhelmed.

Sometimes I notice my own minor irritation at some of the public people I look to for other points of view, inspiration, or ideas. I read the cheerful quips, the encouragements to "go forward!" and I ask myself: While we are indeed nourished by uplifting words, as disasters are happening and world events are unfolding, is "rah, rah, rah" really all we can say in these situations? There has to be something more.

That something, for me, is in the space between giving up and ignoring the pain. That something, for me, is recognizing the power I *do* have and pushing beyond my comfort zone in order to grow and become strong. We can honor our stories and simultaneously try to remember that they are just stories. We can use stories to inform today or use them to get trapped in yesterday or in the false promises of tomorrow. Yes, we live in the context of time and are well served by memory and imagination, but not when these keep us from recognizing what we can do right now.

A plan is helpful. What we've learned in the past is helpful. Hanging on to regret, sorrow, or anger is not helpful. Clinging to some vapor of a dream that we won't put the effort into manifesting is not helpful. Being resigned to "our fate" is not helpful. We are only fated to something if we tell ourselves we are.

What obstacles are you facing? I can give you a whole list of mine. What abilities do you have? What in you feels flexible enough to take on even one of those obstacles, perhaps shifting direction slightly in order to put yourself into different relationship with what feels like an obstruction?

Sometimes the very obstacles themselves are a sign to me that, instead of "go, go, go; rah, rah, rah," what may be more helpful is a change in perspective. For me, this calls to mind the Hanged One of the tarot, who dangles upside down in meditation, waiting until a shift in perspective opens him to the light that breaks through preconceived reality, enabling wisdom to birth itself within. In other words, sinking into patience and opening our field to something new is not the same as resignation. It is active, aware listening to what may be.

This is a difficult lesson about will. At least it feels that way to me sometimes. My personality would much rather have all the answers and know exactly how best to move forward, how best to deliver, and how to make good on the plans I've set in motion, which often involve people who trust me. I hate not knowing, and yet, sometimes, not knowing is how I learn. Not knowing allows the universe to surprise me; it leaves room for the Divine to speak, for the fog to whisper as it leaves droplets on the trees, for the bees to dance the messages only they comprehend. Not knowing leaves room for the weaving of a magic I could not set out to weave were I to plot it carefully.

Engaging will means showing up to work even when we do not know. It means practicing, getting through the list of tasks that we know can be done, making our best attempts with the things that feel like obstacles, and then—most difficult for me— letting some things go for now.

Will is not about a closed fist. Willing is served both by the power To Know and by persistence—by accepting this deep listening state of not-knowing that leads us toward the power To Dare. To put our energy toward something in a way that is appropriate and effective requires discerning when to grip hard, when to hold lightly, and when to let go. The more we persist, the more we practice. The more we practice, the more often we get it right. The more we experience the world anew, the greater our opportunity to know more fully.

MORE ABOUT RESISTANCE

Art begins with resistance—at the point where resistance is overcome. No human masterpiece has ever been created without great labor.

André Gide

We often resist the obstacles that keep us from moving toward our desire, feeling as if we should be on fire for life at all times, listening to those who cheer us on while telling us that nothing is impossible! But some days simply don't feel that way. Inertia takes over. We grow tired or distracted. We feel overwhelmed or mildly depressed. We forget why we made these commitments in the first place—and if we do remember, we wonder what effect we are having and whether or not it is worth all the effort.

This is called resistance. And this is a good thing.

Even while thwarting the flow of life energy, resistance *carries* life energy. If everything felt easy and clear at all times, we wouldn't need will. We would never have to harness our resources and find a way through. In that case, there are things we would not learn and ways in which we would never think to grow.

The butterfly that struggles hardest while leaving the cocoon is the strongest. Sheltered trees are not as strong or as deeply rooted as trees buffeted by heavy winds. Myths always show the ways in which heroes face great challenges and grow. The seed gathers life energy as it forces its way past its hard shell. This gives it the power to climb up through the earth and greet the sun.

Resistance builds muscle. That is a physical fact—and an emotional one as well. But resistance only works if something in us shows up to meet it. That is where will comes in. We don't need much will if everything is always given to us. Under those conditions, to create change requires even greater effort than it does for those who haven't had it easy. Think of how Gautama Buddha or Saint Francis had to renounce lives of wealth and ease in order to grow, learn, and come to follow desire, fulfilling their destinies.

Begin to think of your resistance as both a goad and an ally, rather than as something seeking to drag you into the waters of inertia. Let resistance make you flexible and strong, like the Monterey Cypress trees that stand, wind sculpted, on the California coast. Face desire and resistance to desire. Face yourself. Let each small accomplishment in the face of resistance become a reward for your soul.

When our tasks feel hard, yet we persist, that is a sign of passionate engagement. Something in us simply will not give up. Something in us remains curious about the task, or about the struggle itself. Without this engagement, there is less and less presence. Without presence, it is harder to feel whole—not the wholeness of being finished, of perfection, but the sense that right here and now, we are enough.

The over-culture prefers us asleep. Every effort we make to counter that is a victory. I encourage you to celebrate all acts of persistence and resistance: the run taken, the glass of water chosen instead of soda, the five minutes of meditation, the page written, the closet cleaned, the conversation had. All of these are signs that you are present in the world.

Whatever helps you to persist and resist, even when it feels hard—bless that part of your soul.

BEFRIENDING RESISTANCE

Resistance holds life energy. By giving it a place in our process, we have access to the power it holds. Fighting against resistance expends power. We may as well learn to make it our friend.

Some days, we need to work with our resistance rather than fight against it. There are days when I have scheduled in time to work on a longer project, for example. Since I tend to be a meta-phorical sprinter rather than a marathon runner, large projects can bring up resistance for me. So I fool my resistance. I say "I'm not working on the book, just a blog post," knowing all the while that that post will become fodder for the book, as many of them do. Or I say: "I'll just meditate, do ten minutes of yoga, and then see if I want more exercise." I often do, and those short sessions expand with the addition of other activities, until my body feels happier and stronger.

However, there is a time when push comes to shove and the writing needs to be woven into a book, its structure set, the gaps filled in, and continuity considered. Luckily, there are days when I really am filled with energy and drive and genuinely want to get a move on the work at hand. There are days when I still don't want to get more exercise, but I choose to keep moving anyway, because my health and energy demand it.

What happens when I'm on deadline and my resistance is *still* pulling shenanigans? I find other ways to placate it. I let myself putter just a little bit. I put on my headphones and play some music that is pleasant, but that doesn't engage me enormously. That takes care of the part of me that gets restless. The music gives me something else to pay attention to and lets the rest of me get to work. I allow myself to take little breaks when certain chunks of work get done. Some people bargain around this. I don't find that helpful. Instead, I wait until it feels right, then I make a cup of tea, or step outside, or do some push-ups, or check Twitter for five minutes. Then, break over, I tackle the next section.

We can do this with anything. I get a lot more work done by giving my resistance some space than I do when I try to bind, gag, and bury it. This way, I get to feel engaged with my tasks—connected to creative flow—rather than slogging through chores.

CALL TO REVOLUTION

Art is either plagiarism or revolution.

PAUL GAUGUIN

Resistance, whether internal or external, reminds us that a revolution is coming and that we must find ways to prepare. A revolution is coming and our lives are going to change. No wonder we resist. We may have to drop everything else in order to take a stand. We may even attempt to ignore the call and go back to living lives that are mere copies of what we see reflected around us. We may pretend we didn't hear. Or we may make some attempt to follow, while still getting caught up in the "Why me?" of it all.

Some may even forget there ever was a call. It came, yet was subsumed by the cacophony of sound and emotion that often accompanies life. They did not hear it because the baby was crying, or the dishes needed to be done, or the bills were piling up, or the boss was angry today. Or perhaps at age seven they felt a stirring within them but had no resources upon which to draw. Perhaps at age sixteen they were told that something was a silly dream. Perhaps at thirty they were told it was really time to grow up now. Perhaps at seventy, they were told it was too late.

There is story after story of prophets and mystics who tried to refuse the call, because they felt they were not good enough, or they were frightened of the implications for their lives. There are just as many stories of people who followed that call against all odds. I know both types of people, and often they are one and the same.

Know that it is never too late. We can't copy a revolution; we have to feel the stirrings and decide—Now!—where we stand. When something takes hold—whether it is a simple idea, a feeling, a wish, or a deep and abiding thirst—denying it only serves to give us pain. Yet this very pain is often the medicine and the teacher for our lives. When you hear the call of your soul, what within you feels excitement and what within you feels dread? Pay attention to how you move and what you say, to what needs to be expressed. And this will change over time, because circumstances change.

Following the call changes us—changes something within. And yes, tragedy is always ready to strike, and the laundry does always need to be done. But that does not stop the revolution. The drums are ever beating in our hearts, once the call has come.

PURIFICATION

So-called "negative emotions"—including those that lead to resistance—can be great purifiers. In following our course, We can learn to look at *all* of the emotions at our disposal. Trouble with negative emotions, for instance, tends to come from one of two directions: we either get trapped in them or we try to squash them into non-existence. We either give them pride of place or we diminish and trivialize them. Both of these give our anger, our sorrow, our sense of betrayal or loss far too much power. Both of these methods twist our hearts and souls.

It can be a great help, however, to allow these emotions into our lives so that we can experience them fully and seek the lessons they bring. In this way, anger, jealousy, or sorrow become our teachers and point the way toward greater integration. The fires within that are stoked by these emotions become the fires of purification, lending greater clarity to mind and heart once they have burned through. But this requires staying with ourselves in the midst of difficulty. This requires not running away from ourselves, our emotions, or our thoughts. It also requires not getting fully tangled up in the thoughts and emotions that wish to grab our emotional states and spiral them into a much larger force than they need to become. When we do this, the emotions control us and we are no longer in a balanced relationship with them.

If we are able to feel the strong emotion, however, and stay with it—we can express our relationship to it; opening to the lessons it brings and remaining connected to practice. This is how purification becomes possible.

Purification brings greater lightness, greater connection, and further opening to love. There is nothing in this world that is not part of some greater whole. The sense of disconnection is only our perception. That which makes me angry is a part of me, for we are all part of God Hirself. That which causes sorrow is a part of me, for we are all part of God Hirself.

What would happen to the world if humans engaged in listening and reconciliation instead of war? What would happen to the world if we spoke to the forests and rivers and came to an accommodation so that all forces could run according to some greater good? What would happen if we listened to ourselves in pain, or to our friends, and sought to keep center, boundary, and a sense of connection simultaneously?

It is true that this all takes skill, preparation, and development of the muscles of love and will. We will stumble on our way. But we can learn in this way. Every mistake then becomes, not a failure, but a stepping-stone. In the last chapter, we called our parts back home. Now we will begin cleansing and blessing our relationship to all our parts.

The fires of purification are your friends. Be not afraid. Or hold fear close and enter anyway. That is courage.

Soul Support

Light some candles. Take a breath and gather that which seeks and that which resists. Feel the energy of your desire, and the energy of whatever emotional states are your current companions. As you gaze into the candle flames, invoke your power To Will. Imagine energy building inside you, the energy of fire. Let these emotions, your thoughts, your presence, your practice, and your desire all fan the flames. Feel what within holds you back being slowly burned, burnished, transformed. Let the ashes become fertilizer for the soil in which you will plant something strong. Or let the ashes mix with water, making ink. Feel a divine hand write these words upon your skin: "I will follow this desire. I will live a life that glows

with warmth, passion, laughter, and great love. I invo
pose. I invoke my will. I bless myself, in all my parts.

Sit in the glow of your process and breathe. Feel the p
sibility of all of the energy inside you. When you are ready,
blow out the candles. Feel the warmth that remains.

Action

1. Three days this week, write a letter in dialogue with your
   seeker—that part of you that longs for deeper connection.
   Ask it questions and listen for the answers. Write two to
   three pages, without letting the pen leave the page. One
   question to start you off could be: "Seeker, what do you
   desire?" Pick your writing days now: Monday, Wednesday,
   Friday, or Tuesday, Thursday, Saturday. Know in advance the
   three days you are committing to. A haphazard intention is
   no intention at all.

2. Build an altar to your seeker. Light a candle to your desire.
   Include an object that represents and honors your resistance. Work with this altar over time, letting your relationship to both seeking and resisting grow clearer.

3. Write letters to resistance. Use the same format and structure you used when writing to your seeker. Figure out how
   to become its friend. If you need help with this exercise,
   schedule a session to list things that you consider to be obstacles. Notice if parts of you resist this! Then take a breath,
   and set pen to paper. The Soul Support segments in this
   chapter can help you find a way through.

TRANSITION

THE RITUAL OF WILLING

. . . it is necessary to WILL what is required.

ELIPHAS LÉVI

Do whatever helps alert your soul that you are entering a different space and time than is ordinary for you. You may wish to sit
or stand at an altar, or go to a favorite place outside. Just make
sure you have twenty to thirty minutes of privacy. Have a journal
on hand to make any notes when you return. Have a cup of water
handy to drink at the end, to bring you fully back into the present.
For this ritual, it is also helpful to have a candle, although you can
just imagine one if you wish.

Imagine you can travel to your place of power, your sacred
place—the grove of your heart, the cave of your soul, the temple
of your mind. Relax into your body. Take five deep breaths. Let
each exhalation be another step toward your sacred place. Imagine
yourself entering. What does it look like? Are there trees, ani-
mals, columns, glass, brick, desert vistas, or a night sky? Is there
the scent of plants or of rain on stones? Is there incense burning,
snaking upward? Do ravens call or bells ring? Just notice. This is
your space.

Settle in. Open to your breath. Now notice the energy around you. Notice how the very edges of your skin feel. Bring your awareness to the soles of your feet, the palms of your hands, the very top of your head, your breastbone, and the space between your shoulder blades. Light a candle. Gaze upon it. Feel a corresponding fire just behind the center of your forehead, another ignited in your heart, and yet another in your solar plexus. Then light a fourth flame in your sex. Imagine these flames as a warm glow up and down your body. Feel yourself grow warmer.

Focus on the flame in your solar plexus. Ask yourself: "What is required for me to follow the course of desire?" Feel the flame inside you, and gaze upon the candle. What feeling comes up? What energy takes hold? What are you willing to do? Set an internal intention here, in your sacred place: "I commit to _____, the next step toward the manifestation of my desire."

Next, reach your hands toward the candle flame. Sweep your hands from the candle toward your solar plexus, drawing the power of the flame to strengthen the fire burning inside. Say: "I call in the power To Will. I commit. I will act. I will open to desire."

Let yourself sit and breathe, gazing at the candle, feeling the fire inside and the energy that fills you. Be open to what arises or descends. Stay here for as long as you wish.

When it feels as if it is time to return, thank this place, this time. Bow deeply. Then, on five long breaths, come back to ordinary space and time. Take a breath from the soles of your feet to the crown of your head. Feel the fire that ignites your core. Feel the strength of your intention and your willingness. Blessed be the power To Will.

Extinguish the candle. Take a drink of water. Write down your insights, thoughts, emotions, or sensory input if you wish to. Rest. Be.

You have committed to the next step, which strengthens you and takes you closer to manifesting your purpose.

INVOKING THE NEXT POWER

When we have even a small amount of the power To Will built up, we can begin to exercise the power To Dare. With internal strength and vision from the power To Know, it is easier to face the uncertainty of what is next. We draw upon courage, because we have a sense of resources, inner and outer.

At this juncture, what do you hope for and what do you fear? What is your relationship to desire and your soul? Are you willing to take the risk required to be of greater service to the world, and to your dreams? Breathe into the fire of your will. Stretch your spine. Hold your head with pride. Get ready to face the next challenge. Get ready now, To Dare.

PART III
TO DARE

WE ASK THE WISE COUNCIL:

HOW DO YOU DANCE WITH YOUR RESISTANCE?

It's a constant fight. I use meditation and exercise to feed what I call my "life drive," which is also my drive to create. When I feel empty and listless, I recognize that resistance as my "death drive," which is that part of us that wants to give up and let go. It's only natural; in ancient times, we were lucky to reach the age of thirty. The farther we are beyond that, the more our bodies embody their own type of resistance, which feeds the mental and emotional resistance. Maintaining desire and its healing motivations is a lifelong project.

TANANARIVE DUE

*When it is really bad, I don't. I get rigid about making lists
and checking things off and taking on projects and getting
things done! The part of me that wants to get things done
hijack me. Waking back up to my moist wild trusting desire
self takes small steps and lots of letting go of the story I'm
screwed or a fraud because I let myself get lost again. The idea
from meditation practice of "Begin Again" is hugely helpful.
Remembering the point of being alive is not perfection or
self-improvement but wholeness helps as it is invitation to
love the part of me that deeply believes getting things DONE
is better than sex, rest, or creative truth.*

JENNIFER LOUDEN

*The rhythm of life certainly offers many different avenues for
our mind, body and time. While I remain committed to my
broader life goals, I also realize that in life we need to maintain balance and harmony and for our own well-being, so
that we also understand the world around us—not just the
goal we are striving for.*

MIHIR MEGHANI

*The experiential deep ecology workshops which I facilitate
include Joanna Macy's "despair and empowerment" and other
processes synchronous with the ceremonies and rituals that all
indigenous communities have used throughout time to ensure
that the human family remembers its interconnectedness with
the larger Earth family in which it is embedded. As the facilitator I set the stage but then melt into the circle as a partici-
pant. Having the privilege to participate in such ceremonies
ten or more times each year, I find that my resistance dissolves
again and again. Time in wild nature and actions in defense
of the Earth have a similar effect.*

JOHN SEED

CHAPTER 5

TAKING RISKS

*Learning makes us all uncomfortable . . . Learning tosses each
of us into a state of chaos and our first reaction and desire is
to return to status quo. But to apply the learning and to keep
learning, sometimes we have to stay in the chaos and confusion for a while until we reach a newer and higher level of
status quo. A new level of craft or understanding.*

DEAN WESLEY SMITH[17]

What is the power To Dare? To dare is to risk learning. It requires
courage and attention. Daring can sometimes mean closing our
eyes and leaping into the void, but daring can also mean plotting,
planning, centering, and moving forward in the face of uncertainty.
Daring, when it follows knowing and willing, is a calculated risk.
It is a risk that comes from strength. It is a risk that comes from
some deep connection to ourselves and the wide opening of desire.
Daring is the person walking into the rushing river, holding only a
cup, the third part of the Sphinx.

---

17. Author of numerous novels. You can find his work at
www.deanwesleysmith.com.

I have taken many sorts of risks. Some were unexpected in the moment—heart-pounding and frightening—yet, in retrospect, even those came after many attempts to listen to what my soul wanted. After training and planning, I have also dared to do things that some might not consider risky at all, but that might leave others terrified. In each case, there has been a lot to learn. The learning keeps me going, even when it feels like the most difficult task on earth.

To dare is to court adventure, to explore unknown territory. There is simply no way to know exactly where we are going. All we can see is our next step or two. We may have a map, or a rough outline, or simply a dream. To dare is to be willing not to have things turn out neatly. To dare is to live an uncharted life, mapping as we go. This is filled with excitement and possibility. To dare is to live boldly, to breathe life into our very core, to be willing to shift, to learn, to expand, and to grow.

This is not easy, but it is often fruitful. We will explore the ways in which we can run with courage and daring without being foolhardy strictly for the adrenaline rush of it all. When we have acquired the power To Know and the power To Will, the power To Dare reminds us that our feet are supported by this gorgeous earth, and we live surrounded by expansive sky. Knowledge and willing fuel a daring that is centered, connected, and possibly even joyous. We risk the failure of our own paths toward liberation when we refuse to take the risks that keep us strong.

In the following chapters, we will explore fear, danger, strength, and full presence. Take a deep breath. Feel your body fill with life.

DARING TO DESIRE

Question: How does taking care of our basic needs meet with or deviate from pursuing our desire?

Some of us have likely taken in messages that to want anything beyond what we actually need is selfish or wrong, or does not serve the greater good. I used to feel this way. The guilt of relative privilege coupled with a sense of scarcity marred my attempts to move toward what I really wanted in life—even while I knew simultaneously that following the tugging of my soul was deeply necessary. I lived on little, working odd jobs to pay the rent in order to have time to write, dance, or study. This was good, and yet I also circumscribed what I felt was possible for me. I had some strange version of the American dream: you either make it big or not at all. And since making it big felt too unattainable and was suspect—why would I want to contribute to and be supported by the churning wheels of commerce that crushed others?—I did not let myself really believe success was possible, even while I moved doggedly forward.

It is a testament to the power of desire that, even while doing our best to trip ourselves up, we find ways to return to the deeper sense of what we want and need. We find ways to make it work: taking swimming lessons, carving out time to design new knitting patterns, meeting a friend in a café to write for an hour a week, doing spiritual readings over our morning coffee—on and on our souls find their way toward innovation.

The unfolding of desire doesn't have to be one-pointed, however. That is another myth—that driven artists or scientists must give up every semblance of a "normal" life in order to pursue their craft. I don't believe this is necessary or healthy. The people I know who have followed desire are not only inspiring people I want to be around, they are people whose primary expression of desire is rich and intriguing because they obviously are influenced by many aspects of their lives. Crystal Blanton is part of our Wise Council. Her soul's purpose has led her to work full-time with children in one of the most violent and harsh places in the United States. She also raises a family, writes and edits spiritual books, goes to the gym, teaches workshops on restorative justice, and runs a coven. Her life is rich. She finds ways to care for her body and heart, and to do so under the larger umbrella of her purpose.

My friends who are musicians also create websites, make sounds for movies, work as massage therapists or janitors, and make time to do ritual with friends. My friends who are lawyers also teach political science and ethics, garden, or study North African drumming. One of the key scientists of the 20th century, Carl Djerassi, not only writes books and plays; he also uses the money he made inventing the Pill (among other things) to fund sabbaticals for painters.

The soul cannot be starved if it is to create. Can we dare to deserve desire? Is it "okay" to deserve happiness—to deserve some of what we want as well as what we need? Every time we believe that we deserve to desire, we find ways to feed our souls. How does this happen?

Dr. Sanjay Gupta speaks of being in Pakistan after devastating floods that left so many homeless, sick, and dying.[18] He encountered a girl in a refugee camp doing her schoolwork. Although faced with overwhelming obstacles and surrounded by want and

---

18. This story comes from Dr. Gupta's 2012 spring commencement speech at the University of Michigan.

need, desire had not left her. Something in her knew she was deserving of desire. Her soul desired education, and she was determined to get it.

Can we dare to dedicate ourselves to "the Good" as spoken of by the ancient Greeks? For them, this good was the right ordering of all things, the quality of harmony and balance. To know the good that we desire is to be in touch with our hearts, our souls, our lives. This is known as *eudaimonia*, which translates as "the good spirit," or "fortune." It is not only the way we live; it is how we live well, how we flourish.[19]

PUSHING THROUGH

The force that through the green fuse drives the flower
Drives my green age . . .

DYLAN THOMAS

In chapter 4, we studied the importance of resistance and the power of the shoot pushing through the wall of the seed. Like that shoot, we need the life force to penetrate that which we desire as we seek the warmth of the sun.

When you need to know yourself, nothing will stop you. You will look down every route, climb each set of stairs, and approach every door—although you may not walk far down the route, or scale all those steps, or walk through each portal. Your instincts may tell you to avoid the blue door and go for the green, or you may get halfway up the staircase and run back down again. That is

19. For more on these concepts, see Hannah Arendt's *Life of the Mind* (Mariner Books, 1981) and Aristotle's *Eudemian Ethics* (many sources available).

fine. What matters is this: you are committed enough to yourself and your process to try.

As we take our work with resistance into the power To Dare, we are helped by remembering that we are in a stream of time, ever shifting, ever changing. The narrative doesn't matter much. What matters is that we experience the taste of summer's peach, and listen for the autumnal calling of the crow. In committing to this process, we risk revelation and self-knowledge. We teach ourselves to dare.

We can learn daring by approaching almost anything in our lives. Here are some examples: Writer's block is a lie. The block is placed there by fear—by unwillingness to risk writing for the sake of writing, rather than creating some perfect jewel. The same is true for resistance to sitting meditation. It is yet another risk we must face. Our minds may wander or our backs may ache or we may not feel like better people instantly. But you know what? If you stick with writing, or with the meditation bench, *something inside of you will change.*

Ray Bradbury said that every writer has a million words of garbage inside. Most of us want to bypass that garbage—be it in writing, art, relationships, or work—and get directly to the good stuff. But we can't, because it is *all* "the good stuff" in that it is all necessary to the learning of our craft. I can say the same for the meditation bench. Sitting with myself felt excruciating for at least a decade, but the spirit of inquiry kept me showing up. Sitting, like writing, was teaching me something, even when I was not always certain what the lesson was. I kept at both of them.

Over time, without my really noticing it, writing became just writing and sitting became just sitting, rather than chores or obstacles or things to loathe or fear. Whenever you encounter resistance, ask yourself: Am I willing to dare to do this? If not, what would it take for me to become willing? Is this just the wrong route? If so, why do I keep returning to this pernicious pushing? Why have my thoughts led me to this place yet again? There is something here for me. It may not be the something that will sustain me for the next decade, but I may learn something about myself today.

Soul Support

Commitment is seeded with desire—a wish to be more whole, happy, and useful; more filled with grace, power, or joy. Sit down and listen today. Sink into yourself as you breathe. Feel the space around the body that you inhabit. You! You inhabit that space above, beneath, behind, and to the front. How often do you allow yourself to notice this? How often do you let yourself take up your full width and height? I desire this for you—that you may know yourself and know your worth. I wish that you will take up enough space to reach the sky and tell us what the view is like from there, even as your feet remain planted firmly on the sweet earth. And for those of you who prefer digging to climbing, what lies beneath you? What is turning in the darkness, reaching, or growing, or becoming something new? We ask these questions because curiosity is a sign that we are alive.

DARING PRESENCE

Stay conscious and connected—be aware of your self and your environment at all times as much as possible—and you have the best defense against any danger. You can take calculated risks, avoid unnecessary danger, and live an exciting life every day.

SATYA COLOMBO[20]

In cultivating the spirit of inquiry, we cultivate presence. We learn to listen, to observe; we learn not to make so many assumptions, and not to get caught in so many old patterns and habits.

One of my teachers—the blind seer Victor Anderson—often said: "Anything worthwhile is dangerous."[21] To this, I add the caveat: "But not everything dangerous is worthwhile."

Presence helps us make this distinction. Living with awareness means that any day can be filled with wonder and strangeness. This is not the same thing, however, as running full tilt toward something just because it may be strange or may give us an adrenaline rush. Presence helps us notice more. When we are numb, we miss out on so much. That is why placing the self in different situations often makes us feel more alive—because we aren't operating on assumptions. When we begin to remove assumptions from our day-to-day lives, the fresh possibility of each moment arises.

Presence not only opens us to greater possibility and success; it also enables us to be of greater service. While in a state of presence, for example, I trust the instincts that tell me to turn down this street instead of the next only to see a woman carrying a sick seven-year-old to her car who is clearly going to need help

---

20. Find him at *www.satyacolombo.com*.

21. You can find this and other teachings in *In Mari's Bower* by Cora Anderson (Marion Street Press, 2012) and available through Harpy Books at *www.harpybooks.com*.

unlocking the car doors and getting him settled in. Or I turn my head in time to see a man fall facedown at the escalator leading to the train platform and rush to help him struggle upright. We all have our own stories about following intuition and responding to the moment at hand.

Paying attention to the subtle cues of intuition cultivates presence. Presence puts us in the flow of life, making it easier to dare, because we are working with, rather than against, the flow.

Presence also makes life more interesting to me, giving me days in which I end up rescuing Chihuahuas and bees because of flukes of route and timing, or chatting with friendly anarchist booksellers at a concert I wasn't even certain I wanted to attend. All of this happened between bouts of work, meetings, eating lunch, and going for a walk. All of this happened because I dared to listen to my intuition and follow my inner voice.

CULTIVATING THE PEARL

To dare is to lose one's footing momentarily. To not dare is to lose oneself.

SOREN KIERKEGAARD

Sometimes the energy flowing from will into desire becomes a kernel of irritation within—an itch that needs scratching, or a piece of grit that has the potential to form a pearl. We are struggling to adjust to lives lived via our strengthening desire, and we want the whole world to change—quickly!—right alongside us. When this doesn't happen, the energy that is rising in us needs someplace to go and causes discomfort. This energy can begin to feel like anger, pain, resentment, or even sorrow.

Sometimes I think that trees covered in snow must ache when the sap first starts to rise again. Sometimes I think the shoot must feel bruised during the cracking of the shell. And then I remember once again: the harder a butterfly must struggle to break free from its cocoon, the more robust it becomes. Harsh growing conditions coupled with good care breed stronger grapes.

I find it helpful to ask what the energy beneath strong emotions is trying to tell me. Is there a wish to be heard, a need to make a change, the avoidance of looking at something that frightens me? Do I feel stuck? Is new energy trying to bubble up inside? Is there actual injustice that needs to be addressed, and swiftly? Have I been dragging my feet on some necessary change?

When we train ourselves to listen more deeply, more information rises that is actually useful. When we can sense what else is happening beyond or beneath the pinpoint of irritation or the proximate emotion, we have the chance to free up more energy for our daring journey.

Something new is trying to be born. That process is painful, difficult, and glorious. The sand of irritation is becoming the center of the pearl.

Soul Support

What do you need to dive fully into your desire? What do you need to allow yourself the sweet release of full connection? What do you need to make this commitment to yourself, your life, your work—and to state clearly to yourself first, and then to the world, that this is sacred, this is important, this is an expression of the unfolding pattern of God Hirself?

You are indeed what you have been seeking. No product will give it to you. No sense of outside acceptance will give it to you. No. You have to give it to yourself, from your deepest spaces. You have to take a risk to live your desire.

What in you is still afraid?

Breathe. Open. Find what is at the core of your being. You were born with a fire of connection, a fire for beauty, a fire of the wish to know, a fire of self-expression. Can you be still inside for just this moment? Breathe into your center and relax your edges. Feel how the fire in you—whether a tiny ember or a roaring flame—begins to spread, reaching for the warmth of light around you. You are divine. You have potential. You can make a choice, right now, to walk this earth and live your divine mandate of will, beauty, strength, justice, creativity, and joy. Or you can make a choice to shrink back inside, to hide your fire, never to shine for fear of getting burnt, for fear of outshining someone else, for fear of hurting or feeling hurt. A little pain—the discomfort of growth—is alright. The rewards are greater than your fear.

Embrace fear and tell it: "This will be okay. Life can be better than I even imagine or see from within these fences I've set up for myself." Step toward freedom to answer the calling of the stars as they, even in their dying, exhort you: "Shine. Shine. Shine!"

What will you allow yourself to show the world today? What risk can you commit to, in order to bring more light and fire and beauty to this world? Will you do anything? Will you do everything? The kingdom of heaven is within you, here and now. Spread the word.

Action

The following exercise will help you uncover some of your motivations toward manifestation and some of the reasons you run from it. Don't hesitate to write something down just because it may feel irrational. You need to face all of your parts.

1. Take out a journal or notebook. Write down five to twenty things for which you get positive acknowledgment. List five to twenty things for which you fear punishment or censure. List five to twenty things that give you deep satisfaction.

2. Let these lists "rest" for a week. Look back over them. Do you notice any correlations between the three lists? Are there similarities? What stands out most from each of them? Which feel strongest, or weakest; which feel like old patterns that don't have much life force; which still carry a strong charge?

3. Choose one of the things that you fear and pair it with a thing that gives you satisfaction. Imagine these two things shaking hands. Let the satisfaction in you explain to the fear all of the ways in which you want to manifest your desire. One week later, notice how you feel. Would you like to repeat this exercise with anything else on your list?

CHAPTER 6
GOALS AND CHOICES

One falls to the ground in trying to sit on two stools.
FRANCOIS RABELAIS

The power To Will enables us to set the goals and make the strong choices required by the power To Dare.

When we pursue desire, our goals must become paramount in our lives. We won't be able to make everyone around us happy, and will likely experience discomfort ourselves. When pursuing desire, some of our other activities may have to give way, so that our energies can be harnessed in the proper direction.

Pursuing desire without making our goals paramount is like trying to steer two horses that are intent on going in opposite directions. The chariot slows and grinds to a halt—or worse, topples over, dashing us to the ground. To dare is to engage our will upon the task at hand. To dare is to risk the unknown, which includes the possibilities of both failure and success. We have to risk fulfillment and happiness along with a lot of effort. But when we harness the engine of desire, we become unstoppable.

Gandhi never would have accomplished what he did without daring. Neither would Ida B. Wells, Hypatia, Amelia Earhart, or, to use more contemporary examples, artist and activist Ai Weiwei or the people of Médecins sans Frontières. Without daring, art would not get made and music would not be composed for the rest of us to enjoy. People would labor away timidly and in obscurity, and the world would be the poorer for it.

There comes a time in our quest when daring must enter, or something inside will wither, taking us down the path to atrophy and death. How long can desire languish? A good long time. But the patterns that hold it in abeyance grow stronger in that time, making it all the more difficult to commit the acts of will and daring that can set this part of us free. Daring in this way requires that we choose, that we walk down this fork in the road, that we take a stand, or sometimes that we decide that we've had enough and choose to stay put.

So we show up. We listen. We do our work. We speak. Some exchange happens. Some people will notice. Most will not. That's okay. We don't need to have that kind of a relationship with everyone. Fads will come and go. As long as we are practicing states of connection, we will have something to offer and will be offered something in return. If we continuously reengage with those things that interest us, seek out new things to learn, and share what we find with others, we will ultimately succeed.

What might we dare today? It can be simple or grand—that part does not matter. What matters is that we do something. That we affirm a strong "yes" or state a clear "no." That we sit firmly upon the one chair of our making, or perhaps even stand tall.

THE QUALITIES OF SUCCESS

The founders of Y Combinator, a small venture-capital firm, look for five key qualities when considering the potential success of new ventures: determination, flexibility, imagination, naughtiness, and friendship.[22] These qualities can apply to anything, however, not just financial ventures. Do you want to have a relationship with a lover that is deeply satisfying, with potential longevity? Do you want to improve your physical health? Train your psychic skills? Write books? Make music? Organize a festival? Let's go down this checklist to see what can help you achieve those goals.

- **Determination**: What inspires us enough that we direct life energy toward it on a regular basis—not just making time for it, but firmly placing it in the context of the whole? Is it something we have to do, or is it something we squeeze in? Is it something that we can no longer imagine not doing? Determination keeps our relationship to desire active.

- **Flexibility**: When our projects, relationships, or health throws us a curve, do we care enough to keep daring and respond with flexibility? Or do we give up, take our ball, and go home? How much do we want to create or feel vitality? What is burning at the core that so wants to reengage that we are willing to look at the situation upside down or sideways?

- **Imagination**: We could pen books on this topic, or cloud-gaze and compose a symphony, linking sounds to what we see. Applying imagination to anything can help, whether we are building a house, a partnership, or a mathematical sequence.

- **Naughtiness**: Paul Graham of Y Combinator sees this as rule-breaking. We can speak of it as the ability to move

---

22. For more information on Y Combinator, go to *http://paulgraham.com.*

outside the boxes of convention. In other words, the power To Dare. We need not break rules just to break them, and should know the rules that govern our projects that are needed
to stabilize them. But within those parameters, creativity can flow.

- **Friendship**: This is a reminder that none of us lives or works in a vacuum. I need friends to laugh with, to challenge me, and to act as sounding boards. Friendship sparks connections I just wouldn't experience otherwise. But to be a true friend, I need to keep including all of the other qualities in the list above. Then creativity and feelings of profound satisfaction and joy have a chance to grow.

We can use this list to live the lives we want. I recognize that this last statement is predicated on a certain level of privilege. Let us give thanks for our privileges, large or small, and do our best to live lives that reflect that gratitude. Then let us meet the challenges that life throws at us as best we can and stop throwing more obstacles in our own way.

Often, we get blocked around daring and desire because we lack some of the qualities on this checklist. We may also fail to see ways in which we can approach desire; going through the checklist may help. Rule-breaking is especially germane to risking, because, not only do we sometimes have to break societal rules to get what we want, we may also have to break some of our own family taboos or our own internal rules in order to move in the direction our souls call us.

We all have a lot to offer the world, and the world, in its turn, has much to offer back.

LEARNING FROM FAILURE

Failing helps you see how far is too far, failing helps remind you that failing isn't fatal, and most of all, failing opens you up to succeeding.

SETH GODIN[23]

We all make mistakes. We all have fear of one thing or another, whether that fear is well founded or not. Can you learn to turn your mistakes into lessons? Can you risk regardless of your fear?

Some fear failure; others fear the responsibility of success. Either of these keeps us in stasis, keeps us from pursuing that which we desire. For some, it keeps them from acknowledging desire at all. They close their energy fields, emotions, bodies, and thought processes down so much that they cannot even name what they want, let alone what they desire more deeply.

Each day is an invitation to take another breath into our centers, exhale out, and expand. I'm going to take a moment to do that now. This sense of opening up, of expansion, gives me a larger sense of the space around me. As soon as the animal inside me feels this spaciousness, she settles down, grows less tense and worried. Then she, and the other parts of me, can more accurately assess situations and—more germane to this conversation—catch the scent of possibility.

We don't have to live in tiny rooms within our hearts. We can, day by day, breath by breath, open up to larger vistas. When we feel trapped, it is likely that we've caved in upon ourselves, narrowed our focus, and can no longer see what is outside of us. We have forgotten that we can take the risk of opening a window and seeing the world.

---

23. From his book *Graceful* (New Word City, 2010).

If we are never willing to fail, we are never really willing to succeed. Passionate engagement means that we are learning on the fly, and learning means that we aren't going to get things perfect most of the time. But the reward of passionate engagement is this: We change ourselves over time. One definition of magic is the art of changing consciousness in conformity with will. We have to be willing to allow this change to happen, however. That is the first risk. Who knows what will happen? Not I. Not you. Not anyone—because the moment we open out, the second we expand, a whole new world becomes possible.

Seth Godin, who wrote the words at the start of this section, although hugely successful, has founded many companies that could be considered failures. He, however, considers them to be learning experiences. Godin is filled with passion, desire, and generosity. It is that generosity that keeps him going, I think. For him, the world is not a place of scarcity and competition; rather, the world is a place where innovation is possible, where people can help each other discover better ways of being, of running businesses, of manufacturing, of sharing ideas. He lives from a place of expansion and openness to what can be.

Does Seth ever have bad days? I imagine he does. I certainly do. And it is a rare person who doesn't. But those days, if they come, don't seem to stop what I see as his trajectory of inquiry, engagement, caring, and delight. That's how I want to be—inquiring, engaged, caring, and delighted. Those who develop these qualities can face just about anything: sorrow or joy, success or failure.

Inquiry turns problems into puzzles. Engagement brings us back into active relationship and wonder. Caring opens us up to deeper connection, to compassion, to a wish to be of service to our projects and the world. Delight means we are looking for magic, expecting magic, and finding it in the strangest places.

Yes, I've stumbled, and stumbled hard. I've succeeded and I've failed. I've shown up repeatedly, taking breaths and opening out.

Soul Support

With love, all things are known. With love, your beauty shines. With love, all that you have feared falls away. With love, you rise up, a mighty priestess, ready to take on the mantle of your power. Without love, there is cowardice. Without love, there is fear. Without love, there is oppression. Without love, no justice will be found.

You must now walk in love. This love includes fierceness, strength, and joy. This love includes a sacred defense of what you feel is right. This love means that you stand up for yourself and that we learn to stand together. Because, brothers and sisters, there is trouble in the world.

There have always come times of trouble. Troubled times bring with them huge amounts of energy: the energy of pain, hatred, and anger; the energy of cosmic realignment; the energy of change. You can use this energy to fuel your practice, to fuel your commitments, to fuel your vision, and to fuel your dedication. With this energy, you can light the fires of love and become a beacon to all. With this energy, you can carry the warmth of succor and of inspiration.

What will you choose to do with the emotions and energies of the hardships so many are facing? How—today, right now—can you choose to invoke love in all its forms?

There are those who attempt to steal power without love. We can counter this energy with love and power, joined. We can counter this with the supporting hands of sisters and brothers, the juicy lust of lovers, and the open hearts of friends.

When love takes the reins of power, we become an unstoppable force. We can carry love into every battle we encounter. May our beauty inspire millions.

FACING FEAR

Decide that you want it more than you are afraid of it.

BILL COSBY

Fear is a complex, multifaceted topic. Some fear is obviously a lifesaver. I want to fear getting close to the edge of an actual cliff. I want to fear walking through a strange neighborhood at night. That sort of fear is the animal self telling us to "Pay attention!" And we need to pay attention. We need to find a way to assess situations as accurately as possible.

But what causes us to fear desire? Fear of becoming more fully ourselves? Or perhaps fear of getting trapped in some impractical fantasy world? Or fear of being laughed at by family, friends, or the universe? We don't want to get attached. We want too much to be attached. But desire will out, even if it is the desire to be free of desire. Desire is life in action. Desire is the welling up of a longing that will no longer be denied. It is the whispering—barely heard, but recurring in our ears. Desire is what we seek and what we fear.

Fear helps to bring risk assessment and attention into focus. But how often do we actually do either? In some situations, our animal nature or our rational mind argues with us that something is a risk, and therefore we should avoid it at all costs. The shouts of "Pay attention!" that help in situations of actual danger become instead a way to ignore what is really happening around us, focusing our attention instead on the emotions fueling the fear. We start to see monsters lurking in closets where there are none. We start to choreograph spectacular failures that we just know will happen. Fear becomes a cage.

But fear is both the cage *and* the key.

I often say that everything in life is about relationship, and every relationship entails risk. Facing risk is part of how we grow; it is how we learn new things; it is a way to engage our curiosity so we can say "I wonder how this works," or "I wonder what might happen if ..."? Below, I write about running toward danger. This practice has enlarged my courage, my ability to learn, and my heart. Yes. I risk more in relationships now. This doesn't mean that I engage in "risky relationships," however. Rather, it means that I take more risks in the relationships that are important to me.

What helps with this? Again, that phrase "I wonder ..." My past, my emotions, my old thought forms still want to manufacture "I know ..." attitudes when actually I don't know yet. This freezes my words and actions. Recognizing that this is just fear helps me to understand that, in most cases, fear points to something that feels dangerous—emotionally dangerous, or dangerous to my parts that like to know the outcome of things before they begin, or dangerous to the parts that would rather sit in bed and read all day rather than confront a difficult truth. By recognizing that this is just fear, I can actually assess the situation and say: "What is actually happening here? Oh. I feel afraid. All right, I can re-center, breathe, and find energy to back up the words I need to say, or the questions I need to ask." Facing these sorts of fears helps to deepen intimacy in my relationship with myself, with my friends and loved ones, and with the world.

I even think it makes me a better person. It also helps me to walk through a strange neighborhood at night and more accurately assess real danger, rather than populating the streets with phantoms that may not exist. It enables me to shift my posture to one of confidence. That makes it less likely that what I fear will actually come to pass.

Fear can help us. Fear can also box us in. We have to learn to trust ourselves to know which kind of fear is which. Fear cannot become the driver of our carriage, nor its master. But we can listen when the horses tell us they feel spooked and decide whether to turn the corner or to reassure them that the driver knows the way—or that we are willing to take responsibility for not knowing and move forward anyway.

RUNNING TOWARD DANGER

In my life, I have long been running toward danger—running toward what I fear, what forces me to expand, what challenges me, what busts up my life and reshapes it in a new way. Over time, I have grown strong enough and supple enough so that the reshaping looks gentler and less like the toppling of a great tower than the raising of a beautiful new city. The city is my life, my soul, my relationships, my work. The city is my self.

Someone once asked me if I have people sign waivers for my classes that include physical activity. When I said "No," she naturally wanted to know why. My answer was this: "Most of the danger is within."

As was discussed previously, fear is natural and often a helpful teacher. It can keep us from the sort of danger that ends in trauma. But sometimes we listen far too much to fear and worry. Are we going to risk the results of numbing and swaddling our souls? Or are we going to risk that which is barely known, that for which the soul reaches?

My training in nonviolent intervention showed me that I had to retrain my instincts to run toward the sounds of fighting rather than away. That was the only way I could ascertain whether or not I could be of help, whether or not it was any of my business, whether or not the right thing to do was to interpose my body or my voice between one person and another. I've stopped large men with weapons, teens choking each other over drug money, a grown man threatening his elderly mother, and a beating on a dark street at night.

Learning to do this for others helped strengthen me to do this for myself. Part of me has always run toward the danger of gnosis and toward the difference that would set me apart from most of my peers growing up. Yet, fearing interpersonal conflict, I shrank away from my own defense. Parts of me always resisted and tried to constrict into a ball and hide to avoid conflict or hurting someone's feelings. Parts of me tried to be a little less bright than I was. This did not serve my soul, although it taught me lessons I hope never to forget.

Self-preservation is a good thing, but not when it comes at a price so high we can barely comprehend it. What is the self we are trying to protect and preserve? Is it the self that has the best interests of our brave soul at heart? Or is it the self that lives in worry and fear, that wants to protect us from our brilliance, our power, and our glorious beauty?

The people who inspire me have all run toward danger. They have all been willing to take the risks that form art, that seek justice, that shape the spirit in breathtaking ways. They have risked the silence of meditation. They have risked the exposure of asking for what they really want. They have risked stating an opinion or standing up for a deep belief. They have traveled the world, seeking mystery, or they have stayed at home in prayer and study. They have danced around fires. They have fed children. They have sat down, arms linked, in front of riot police. They have written poems and sung songs and painted canvases. They have spoken out. They have looked their demons in the eye. They have done the work to grow toward wisdom. They have grown into themselves—fully present, fully sacred, fully alive.

STARTING WITHIN

> *It is for us to pray not for tasks equal to our powers, but for powers equal to our tasks, to go forward with a great desire forever beating at the door of our hearts as we travel toward our distant goal.*
>
> HELEN KELLER

Without an abiding desire that brings us back to the search for that desire again and again, external praise can lead to internal failure. No outside confirmation is lasting. The only thing that lasts is what is accrued on the inside. Success is granted within.

Sometimes we just want external validation on our journeys. I'll take myself as a case in point. Periodically, I get an itch to go to graduate school. I had been preparing for this right before my first book was published and my life was turned on its head. Needless to say, I dropped the project, because it seemed life was taking a different course. However, there is still something in me that loves to study, loves the intellectual sparring with others, and wants more training. There is also a part of me that wants the external validation of some letters tacked onto the end of my name. When I look at the amount of time and effort and money a PhD requires, however, I usually find other places to channel my energy. The external validation is just not strong enough to fuel my desire.

External validation never satisfies our cravings for very long. In the book *Art and Fear*, the authors talk about an artist whose driving goal was a one-person show at a prestigious gallery.[24] He worked toward that day, year after year. Finally, the show opened to great acclaim. Success! You know the punch line to this story, right? He never really painted again. His painter's soul had turned into a soul that wanted outside recognition and proof of his worth. The soul that loved painting itself gave up somewhere along the way, subsumed by this other goal.

Why do we apply ourselves, if not for the love of the work? Even those who have a clear outside goal going in must want to engage fully for the love of it; otherwise they end up over and over with half-finished projects or haphazard practice only to return to something easier. Inner desire engages our will to its fullest for the long haul. What interests you about your study? What interests you about your partners or children? What interests you about painting, music, dance, gardening, or physics? What interests you about magic, about meditation, about plumbing the depths of your soul and seeking out your heart's desires?

When we rely on external pursuits, there are too many variables. Circumstances change and will always do so. We change inside as well. But our internal changes are things we can keep track of. When I am in active relationship with my internal goals and processes, it is quick and relatively easy to make slight adjustments in my course when things around me fall apart or look different close up than they did from far away.

---

24. David Bayles and Ted Orland, *Art and Fear: Observations on the Perils (and Rewards) of Artmaking* (Image Continuum Press, 2010).

It takes daring to rely on ourselves and our deep calling, rather than seeking outside confirmation or approval. But all of the great people whom we admire and look to for inspiration did just this. They followed what was in their hearts and minds, often facing great resistance from those around them. They found the courage somehow to move with and strengthen the wish inside.

Remember our ordinary heroes? Sometimes courage manifests in moments of great daring; but most days, courage looks like showing up to the task at hand, even when you feel you do not want to. We have to face the fear that keeps us from our goals and say, in clear voice: "I choose this anyway."

EMOTIONAL DARING

> *There is a vitality, a life-force, an energy, a quickening that is translated through you into action and because there is only one of you in all of time, this expression is unique. And if you block it, it will never exist through any other medium and be lost.*

> Martha Graham

We've reached a point where the known doesn't cut it anymore. We've delved into knowing and developed will. We've rested and regrouped. Now it is time to face the unfamiliar. We can't play it safe, staying with the known. We have to take the risk.

Daring doesn't have to look like an active, headlong rush forward. Sometimes it is just the opposite. If we are always rushing forward, perhaps daring requires us to sink, to soften, to open out toward deeper states of listening. For example, at the time of this writing, I'm in my middle forties. I've been pretty *yang* for most of my life: active, macho, bold, opinionated, an instigator, a starter. This is shifting. These qualities aren't going away per se, but I find that I'm being called upon to learn more about my *yin* qualities: softening, waiting, slowing, deepening. I feel a need for less fire and more water—and not even the powerful, terrifying water of large waves on the ocean, but the deep, still waters of a sheltered lake. This requires daring on my part, because these things are less known to me. I trust that they must be included. I open my heart, mind, and soul to receive.

There is no reason not to move toward that which we desire, even when this requires a new relationship with our emotions. Yes, there are obstacles to overcome. Yes, there are parts of self to integrate and bring on board. Yes, sometimes things seem frightening or difficult. But what have we got to lose? The stakes are high, but what will we lose by refusing to take the risk? We risk everything, really, because we risk our hearts, our souls, and our Divine Work. We may as well move forward, wading into the water, cup held high.

A STORY ABOUT DARING

Referring to the words of Martha Graham above, Lisa, who attended one of my Courting Desire classes, wrote:

> As empowering as this quote is, it is also scary. It feels like such a large task to take on, totally expressing who I am when I've had to keep who I am bottled up for so long in order to survive in the dysfunctional family I was born into. I do want to express and not block my life force energy and creative flow. I am not sure exactly how I am blocking it,

but I know that most of the time, it is not flowing freely. Yes, there are times that I can get really focused and do something creative, but more often than not, I sit in a room filled with yarn and fabric and can't decide what materials I want to use and what I want to shape them into. It can all feel so overwhelming at times.

I replied: "Sometimes you just have to start."

Soul Support

Where do emotions reside in your body? Chest, neck, shoulders, abdominal muscles?

After you read this, close your eyes, take a long, slow breath, and sink into the space just beneath your navel. Think about desire, about your soul's work, about success or failure or magic. Notice what happens in your body. Is it tension? Relaxation? Anticipation? Butterflies? Is there a sense of excitement? Of fear? Of some other energy or emotion? Stay with this for a moment.

Now imagine that just around you is a field of energy that follows the contours of your skin—your etheric body—and that farther out around you is your shining body—the egg sometimes called the aura. Take in another breath and imagine your exhalation "pushing" both these fields out another two inches or so. This gives your emotions more space. Notice if some tension in you relaxes. Start to breathe in more life, consciously filling yourself with strength and the ability To Dare.

Action

1. Look at your life, as it is. Imagine as much detail as possible. Now imagine you are a stranger encountering your life for the first time. What do you notice? Are there patterns you see? Different things that pop out on the surface or settle just underneath? What would you think of yourself and your life if you could see with a new pair of eyes and hear with different ears?

2. Go through this list: determination, flexibility, imagination, naughtiness, friendship. Write down your relationship to each of these words. How well are you including each of these qualities in the manifestation of your purpose and the following of desire? What changes can you make in your life—returning to the power To Will—in order to align with these qualities better and lead a full, productive life?

3. Find an image that represents support for your daring. Frame it and hang it up where you can see it daily. If music works better for you, find a song you can listen to a few times a week. During one big life transition, I listened to "More" by the Sisters of Mercy with great regularity. It bolstered my courage to begin to ask more clearly for what I actually desired.

4. Set a timer for five minutes and complete one of these statements: "I am willing to risk . . ." or "I dare because . . ." Don't let the pen stop moving until the time is up. What surfaces?

TRANSITION
THE RITUAL OF DARING

. . . it is necessary to DARE what must be attempted.

ELIPHAS LÉVI

Once again, do whatever helps alert your soul that you are entering a different space and time than is ordinary for you. You may
wish to sit or stand at an altar, or go to a favorite place outside.
Just make sure you have twenty to thirty minutes of privacy. Have
a journal on hand to make any notes when you return. For this
ritual, have some water nearby. If you have a favorite cup or chal-
ice, that would be appropriate for this rite.

Imagine you can travel to your place of power, your sacred
place—the grove of your heart, the cave of your soul, the temple
of your mind. Relax into your body. Take five deep breaths. Let
each exhalation be another step toward your sacred place. Imagine
yourself entering. What does it look like? Are there trees, ani-
mals, columns, glass, brick, desert vistas, or a night sky? Is there
the scent of plants or of rain on stones? Is there incense burning,
snaking upward? Do ravens call or bells ring? Just notice. This is
your space.

Settle in. Open to your breath. Now notice your emotions. Notice what burrows beneath the depths or soars above. Look at the cup in front of you. Hold it in your hands. Imagine that there is another cup in your chest that holds all the qualities of your heart: openness, love, fear, courage, timidity, strength, grief, resilience, or joy. Send a breath through your chest, from back to front, allowing it to ripple the waters, bringing a greater sense of ease and awareness.

Remember what you know and what you will. Ask yourself: "What do I dare?" What inside you longs for daring? What wishes to be bold and take a risk toward greater fulfillment of desire? Pour a small amount of water into your hands. Trace the water across your face, your neck, your breastbone. Say out loud: "I call in the power To Dare! I call in my ability to choose, to risk, and to open the gates of passion and desire!" Let the power of daring wash through you.

Stay with this for as long as you wish.

When it feels like time to return, thank this place, this time. Bow deeply. Then on five long breaths, come back to ordinary space and time. Take a breath from the soles of your feet to the crown of your head. Feel the liquid that washes through your heart. Feel the openness and bravery of daring. Blessed be the power To Dare.

Drink the remainder of your water. Write down your insights, thoughts, emotions, or other impressions if you wish to. Rest. Be.

INVOKING THE NEXT POWER

Call upon your ability to contain the energy and momentum you've been developing via the powers To Will and To Dare. Harnessing the powers of intention and our emotions brings us to a place of consolidation. Daring opens our hearts. Silence gives this new relationship a chance to settle. You now get a chance to reassess, to incubate, to grow strong as you contemplate how best to move toward manifestation.

Find the stillness in your center. Call to yourself the power To Keep Silence. Breathe deeply. Let's begin.

PART IV

TO KEEP SILENCE

WE ASK THE WISE COUNCIL:

WHAT ROLE DOES SILENCE OR CONTEMPLATION
HAVE IN YOUR PRACTICE OR WORK, OR IN FOLLOW-
ING DESIRE?

*It's extremely important to me. As a child in my first years of
school, I didn't speak English. So most of my recess time was
spent alone, in my own world. I never once felt any sense of
loneliness. But later in life, I realized that this experience was
absolutely crucial. In a way, it formed my very world, the
very essence of who I Am. I continue to spend most of my time
alone, and am very rarely lonely.*

ANAAR

Every morning, I do a contemplation to prepare myself for the day. I practice Surat Shabda Yoga. It is a way to "reset" myself and seek neutral ground from which an evolving perspective can easily manifest and articulate itself through my attitude, attention and awareness.

DANA REASON

Careful consideration of my role as a clinical counselor and the needs of those I serve is paramount to being a professional and doing this job to the best of my ability. Keeping a professional distance between myself and my client often takes conscious consideration and reflection, as well as silence. The work I do is not about what I want for a client but instead supporting a client in finding out what he or she wants for his or herself. To be silent and to listen might just give someone the chance to be heard in a way that has not happened before. This is a great gift in learning to balance my own desire to be of service and knowing that my service might just mean allowing others to find themselves.

CRYSTAL BLANTON

I was once driving back home in the late afternoon when I realized that, by driving off into the fields, I could watch the sun set over the magnificent Nimbin Rocks. So, I took a track to the east, crossed a creek culvert and sat on the hillside watching the glory. Driving back down much more slowly, as I reached the bottom of the hill, I noticed a Rainforest Dove in the middle of the causeway pecking at seeds that had fallen from the trees that lined the creek. Suddenly I realized that just being human didn't give me the right-of-way, she was there first. So I stopped the car, turned off the engine and relaxed, enjoying the trees and the bird and the stillness. Eventually she had eaten her fill and took flight. As I reached for the key to turn on the ignition, the trees erupted in a cacophony of birdsong.

JOHN SEED

Chapter 7

THE ALCHEMY
OF SILENCE

My son, be silent! Silence has many beauties.

Sophocles

The power To Keep Silence is deep. This is not the silence of suppression or oppression, nor is it the silence that comes from fear of telling our truth. The power To Keep Silence is the power of the stones and the gestating seed, the power of incubation and unspoken mystery. Silence takes all of our thoughts and experiences and gives them the space to be. It is only through being that we can learn the deeper truths of life and be shown our purpose more clearly. This unfolding takes time. The power To Keep Silence is supported by the steady strength of the bull, the fourth part of the Sphinx.

To manifest our work in the world, we often think we must always be in a state of fiery will—that we must "Go! Go! Go!" This is a sure road to burnout, dissipation, and failed dreams. Before we can fully manifest what we desire—let alone enact our lives' purpose—we must take time to rest, contemplate, and regroup. Just as important as these is another facet of silence: digestion and integration. Without space and time to allow what we have done and learned to percolate fully into all parts of our being, we aren't really doing anything in the long term other than running around making noise. We may have temporary successes, but unless we allow silence to change us, we will keep making the same mistakes or even having the same kinds of results. Over time, even the same good results start to look like mistakes, because nothing substantial has been altered within us. If we do not change, our work fades.

Similarly, without the ability to hold our projects close to our breasts, we are always scattering our creative energy far and wide, never having enough power to consolidate and make something fine, something new, something potent. If we speak about our process to all and sundry, not only does a part of us think we have already accomplished this thing—and therefore don't need to put in the hard work needed—we also scatter the very fuel that we need to harness our will and get moving once again. In other words, without silence we undercut ourselves, wear ourselves out, and fail to reach our deeper goals. We only make flashy magic, and never bring forth the magic of real import. Our impact diminishes.

COURTING SILENCE

Learning how to be still, to really be still and let life happen—that stillness becomes a radiance.

MORGAN FREEMAN

When we allow more silence and presence into our lives, we are offered a greater chance to sense desire. A life filled with clamor, noise, worry, and rushing is a life most often lived in the midst of conflicting wants and needs. Courting silence, therefore, helps us to court desire more effectively.

This growing silence will not be very silent at first, until all of our parts grow used to the process of dropping into our core and submerging into stillness. Over time, however, our very connection to self can change in this space. We can cultivate a greater sense of who we are that is not enmeshed in our identity or the push and pull of family, school, work, and expectations. A clearer sense of ourselves as Beings has a chance to emerge from the depths. That deeper sense of self often brings with it the kernel at the heart of our desire.

Until this point, both desire and our souls' purpose may feel nebulous, in conflict with our lives, or not present at all. From stillness and silence, however, we can begin to touch the edges of our lives' purpose with sensitive fingertips. We can hear it whispering and will wonder how we missed its voice before. All of a sudden, from the place of stillness at our core, we will feel the tugging insistence of destiny.

What is it? What wants to draw us forward from this place of sitting still?

We cannot move until we know the power of stillness. There is no music and no speech without the silent void from which all sounds arise.

Soul Support

Remember that, in your center—your core—there is a place of stillness like a deep pool of water. In your mind, hold a smooth stone. Write upon that stone: Silence. Let it drop into that pool; see it moving down, down, until it is submerged in darkness. Feel the stillness ripple out into your being. Just sit. Breathe. As thoughts, emotions, or distractions arise, let them also drop into the pool. Court the silence in your body. Let the edges of your skin begin to feel a lightness and an opening. Deep core; light edges.

Now listen. Let the silence become a place of deeper listening. This is a listening beyond thought, beyond sound, beyond preconception. This is a listening for what is and what can be. Sense the rising stillness of desire. Like sun breaking through clouds; suddenly, the light does change.

BEFRIENDING MYSTERY

Let us be silent, that we may hear the whispers of the gods.
RALPH WALDO EMERSON

Finding our purpose involves a certain amount of mystery. The Mysteries, according to ancient tradition, can never be spoken, but only revealed. The injunction toward silence conveys that there are some things that words simply cannot impart. The Mysteries can only be revealed to initiates when they are ready. Silence both prepares us to receive the power of mystery and makes space for mystery to open in our lives.

Without space to sink and open into, the unknown, desire, success, love, and work often end up feeling bewildering. We may not be sure why the effort we expend isn't paying off as we want it to. We may wonder at the good fortune of our friends: are they really doing anything differently from us? We may end up pushing harder, working more, and expending greater amounts of will.

Meanwhile, we are ignoring the calling of the sacred silence. We are ignoring the deeper needs of heart and soul.

Magic requires room in order for our wishes to be met. While knowing, willing, and daring are all important to the operation of magic and creativity, allowing for silence brings things to a fruition that is often less expected, deeper, and richer than what our minds imagined. Silence and gestation give the less insistent parts of self a place in the process. They also allow room for the cosmos and divinity to work with us. We do not know it all and we cannot do it all. Magic happens in the spaces left between will and daring: mystery flows in, creating something new.

This lesson has not been learned easily by me. My tendencies are to be a highly opinionated doer, who always knows the best way. Training toward greater openness, silence, and curiosity has required conscious effort on my part; it has also come about because, somehow, in my periods of not knowing, the tugging of desire and destiny kept me going anyway. This was true even in those brief phases when all I wanted to do was lie around and read novels. What helped me through? The fact that surprising things still happened, showing me that there was more going on in the universe than I could possibly account for.

Years went by, and here I am—a teacher, mentor, author, and world traveler. All of these are things the working-class poor girl I was would never have expected. I had daydreams of being an author, but never would have planned the rest. The unexpected manifested partly through my effort, and partly because I was willing to allow for mystery to grow.

These days, I court stillness and spaciousness more and more. It helps. Something is coming for me. I don't know what it will look like, but I aim to be ready to meet it when it arrives. The mystery and I, we have become old friends.

CULTIVATING DESIRE

Question: Can we locate the seed of a desire within us and intentionally cultivate it in order to bring us to a new place in our lives?

Courting silence and befriending mystery help us cultivate the seed of desire. They help us see, feel, touch, hear, and taste more clearly. Sometimes the seed of desire can be found through a flash of insight. Most often, however, it requires a settling into self and touching something larger than that self in order to see that our purpose comes from connection. Our purpose is fed by and feeds connection in its turn.

Like mammals, seeds require gestation, the time to go through the subtle processes necessary for growth. Our constant movement is like pulling plants up in order to see how they are growing. Those plants will never properly root, and eventually will die. In this way, the power To Keep Silence is woven through all the other powers. The greater our ability to maintain connection to our still center within, the more deeply we will acquire the power To Know, the better able we will be to exercise the power To Will, and the easier it will become to know when to invoke the power To Dare. Silence teaches us about what matters in the long run.

To cultivate desire and grow purpose more effectively, accept the invitation silence offers. Let the seed nestle in the earth. Water it. Shine light upon the soil. Feed it nutrients. The basic things you do to lead a healthy life can nurture the seeds of desire. Pray, exercise, eat well, rest, play, work, and take in inspiration. Hold space, and allow time for the gestation of mystery. When you get used to this process, all of a sudden, time itself becomes your ally. How many of us are in a constant fight with time? More rushing does not help this relationship. Only slowing down or sometimes even stopping shifts the scales.

Do not mistake stillness and silence for apathy or inertia. Apathy swaddles us in cotton wool. Stillness cleanses the soul. Stillness connects us to the pregnant silence of darkness, where something fine is waiting to be born. Hold this. Hold yourself.

SLOWING DOWN

> *For I am divided for love's sake, for the chance of union. This is the creation of the world, that the pain of division is as nothing, and the joy of dissolution all.*
>
> NUIT, THE STAR GODDESS[25]

We worry; we attempt to fix things; we get things done. We also need to slow down. I say this to my students all the time: Don't ramp up your energy inside to match the energy outside. If you want to get things done effectively, slow down.

Sometimes, however, even I forget—despite my words and practice. One day, in dealing with some crises, interrupted sleep, a stack of work, and knowing I would be out of town all the next week, I sped up inside and sent an email that tried to convey a simple need and failed. Why? Because I did not slow down enough to listen properly. I let a businesslike tone try to speak when a more human, more honest missive might have communicated better. It was not a big deal, and my colleague and I worked it out, but it points to a lesson for me nonetheless.

---

25. From *Book of the Law* as transmitted through Aleister Crowley. Many editions are available.

There is division within us, within me. And that division gives me a chance to learn lessons. There is struggle, despite the perfection of Nuit in all her starry, unified splendor. Most of us get caught in the division and that causes pain. It doesn't have to.

Sometimes we try too hard—we force the issue, the body, the mind, the situation. When we allow ourselves to open, to soften, to come into awareness, things arise that we never saw before, and information comes to us that the front of the brain simply cannot access in isolation. Where is the silent earth within?

As of this writing, my morning practice of yoga before meditation continues. Will I ever flow into the downward dog posture like one member of our Wise Council, the talented Suzanne Sterling? I feel doubtful. My hamstrings, always tight, perniciously refuse to release my legs enough for my heels to touch the mat while in that pose. And yet, every morning, I show up, because I want to be reunited with God Hirself, flowing into all—however imperfect that connection may seem to me. I want to become one with my body again after a night in bed—sleep or no sleep. I want to remember that movement and stillness are one thing, and that breath unites them. Am I in competition with myself to see whether or not my downward dog will improve? No, strangely enough for one who used to be as macho as I was. I am curious to see whether or not I will keep showing up for this devotion to practice, connection, and opening. The patient struggle of yoga leads me into the dissolution of identity in the meditation that follows.

Perhaps ten years from now, yoga itself will cease to feel like a struggle, just as the meditation finally did. I don't know. I really don't care. Practice has become an act of love, offered to my learning process, to my shifting state of humanity. The mat and the meditation bench are altars. I become both the offering to the Gods and the offering to my own divine nature.

A Story about Slowing Down

One day, I was listening to the rain and began to notice how a sense of quiet had softened me. I felt the rain ask questions to which only my soul knew the answers—my mind not being soft enough to comprehend. When I opened to the rain, a lightness occurred in my solar plexus, and a gentle expansive waving of connection surrounded my body. That day, I wrote this:

> The form opens to that which has no boundary but that of association. The water is in motion. So am I. And in this motion, something in me feels quite still. This stillness does not come from pointed focus, but from a diffuse sort of grace. I am alive, and it is raining. Flowers rejoice.

Soul Support

What inside you can slow down today? What can breathe and look at the pain and joy of division? What can you offer at your altar, for love's sake, for a chance of union? Silence is with you: in the downtown city streets, in the frantic checking of news and websites, in worries about friends, clients, children, or this world. Can you sense it? Can you feel it?

What is your offering? Can you bring some silence, slowness, and devotion to your work today? What is divided in you, and what unites? Slow down for a moment and simply be.

TRUSTING

> *The inability to open up to hope is what blocks trust, and*
> *blocked trust is the reason for blighted dreams.*
>
> ELIZABETH GILBERT

Silence allows us to listen, and listening brings us into a state of trusting. We learn to trust ourselves better when we listen deeply, because our thoughts and emotions are better informed and not running around crazed with energy and suppositions. We learn to trust the world and our responses to the world, because our interactions with the world are more and more based upon what we actually see, sense, hear, taste, touch, and know, instead of what we think we should see or what our emotions tell us about how things have been before. We can face the world fresh—with experience, yes, but not with overly programmed assumptions or knee-jerk reactions.

We come to know others better through listening, and feel seen, heard, and known ourselves when we are listened to. The listening I write of here is not the hypervigilance that trauma or abuse survivors often experience. I have some of that in my history as well—contributing to noise sensitivity and light sleep— because the child I needed to listen to know whether or not things were safe. That survival technique is a type of listening that causes constriction, rather than opening and deepening into silence. When we learn to listen in this other way, we can trust our friends, bosses, and teachers better, because we come from our deep and centered places and can better assess what they are offering. If our deep self warns us not to trust, the information is more likely to be accurate.

MAKE MAGIC OF YOUR LIFE

Separation is an illusion. Sometimes it is a joy to feel our edges bump against the edges of other people in heated conversation, laughter, healing, or a kiss. And sometimes, this sense of otherness causes us severe pain—a disengagement that wounds whole countries, rends families, and seeds the base of Everest and the space between the earth and stars with garbage. Despite this, we can come together by recalling that we are never really apart.

God Hirself divided—for love's sake, for a chance of union. We all have been divided for love's sake and can come together once again. We are All. We are All Right. We are climbing the sacred mountain, picking up the garbage as best we can.

We began our process with the power To Know, but here we see that it is only by entering the power To Keep Silence that we can know on more profound levels. The dictum "Know thyself" requires many passes through the Powers of the Sphinx, and the power To Keep Silence is a potent phase that ends up informing everything else. It enables us to grow as human beings, as makers of magic, as manifesters of our deep desires.

A Story about Trust

One morning, reading the BBC news caused me to head to my altar and hold the world in love and meditation. I was feeling the pain and trouble in the world, yet there was simultaneously a sense of peace and well-being within me. There was the sense of everything being "All Right." There was still a flow from me to the giant sycamores outside and to the people in the cars or on bicycles that passed beneath them. I felt the privilege of Being—here, on this planet, in this cosmos, at this time. I realized that the gratitude I felt came from the state of connection and bliss that is available to me whenever I choose to remember: it is Now.

Later that day, there were plenty of volunteers at the soup kitchen, so I left early in order to get some work done before my afternoon and evening spiritual-direction clients. Riding my bicycle down the hill, I thought: "I wonder if Jerry is in the shop." Jerry is a friend who was in a terrible auto accident and had been unable to work since then. Trusting my intuition, I took a chance, and there he was. After catching up a bit, I offered to do some energy work with him. Fifteen to twenty minutes later, we stopped and looked at each other—he with cathartic tears on his face and I with peace in my heart. We had experienced a full connection with each other during the healing. The current flowed in all directions, linking us in a place of deep listening with each other, with the whole shop, with the people who came in to browse, with . . . God Hirself, the limitless All.

Soul Support

To reconnect to the flow of all things, remember that you are not alone, and that support is right beneath your feet. This gorgeous earth is a companion on your journey. You are part of earth, and earth is part of you. We are made of star stuff; our molecules are intertwined.

Stand or sit as tall as you can, feet flat on the ground if at all possible. Find your center and circumference. Breathe for a few moments. Then begin to imagine that you can exhale through the soles of your feet, opening them further to what is beneath you. Stay here for one breath, attention dropped.

When you feel ready, imagine that you can breathe up your connection to earth through the soles of your feet and into your core. Then imagine you can exhale through the crown of your head. Reach for the vast possibility above you, and the welcome opening of sky. Remain here for one breath, with your attention expanded. When you feel ready, imagine you can draw down the vast openness of sky, inhaling through your crown and into your core.

Just breathe, feeling the energies of earth and sky mixing in you. Allow your soul and body to feel connected to the sacred here and now.

When you feel ready, inhale through feet and crown simultaneously, and exhale through every pore of your skin. Do this three times. You are connected. You are alive. There is no separation unless you choose to feel that way.

STILLNESS AND MOTION

The thing that rants and raves and seeks, make it still. That thing that never moves, make it move.

KOYOTE THE BLIND[26]

When we ignore the power of stillness and fall into the trap of constant motion, we leave ourselves open to an endless grind of self-diminishment and the diminishment of others, which only wastes energy we could be applying toward will and change. This often masks deeper problems or fears, or a wish to remain stuck rather than risking opening to flow.

---

26. You can find his work at *www.koyotetheblind.com.*

The power To Keep Silence makes you strong. Be still, and know that you are God. Then take that divine impulse and run. Joyously.

A Story about Stillness

A few years ago, I made a commitment to the cosmos to step up my responsibility and open further to power. As life has it, this also included my time at the gym. I knew I needed to be healthy to strengthen my will and that I had to strengthen my will to become healthier.

I took on the practice of not complaining at the gym as a way of containing and focusing my energy rather than wasting it. So I forewent little self-deprecating, funny comments or saying I was going to die when clearly I was not. I practiced acting on the prescription in the Koyote quote above. It helped a lot. But my mind was still quick to go to "I don't like this" or "I can't do this" before I could see it, take a breath, re-center, and shift my attention to something that felt more helpful. We all have our old patterns, and this is one of mine. Even after years of working to expand my capacity on all fronts, the diminishment of power can insinuate itself into my mind. So on the day in question, I pushed through the workout, engaging within and then collapsing within, then re-engaging, then re-collapsing.

As we cooled down, my trainer observed that she saw the strength in my body, could watch when I got a thought, and then sensed my energy start to spiral down. "What does this tell you?" she asked. "That the mind is a powerful thing," I replied.

Committing more fully to my life and to my soul's purpose—the Work of This God—included committing more fully to my workouts. I had to bring all of my meditation and energy practices to the bench, to the rack, to the mat, to the street, to the park. The thing in me that rants? It must be held in abeyance and taught to become still. The thing in me that never moves? It must move. For magic workers, nothing is outside the realm of practice.

In working with my trainer, I was teaching myself the ways in which the power To Keep Silence helped to bolster both my self-knowledge and my will. Without the practice of silence, I would not have learned nearly as much about the workings of my mind and energy. My attempts to engage will would have become a rote pushing forward instead of a deepening engagement.

Soul Support

Feel this. You are a living, breathing being in a living, breathing world. You pulse with the air and the sun and the sky. You pulse with the microscopic organisms and the radiant stars. You pulse with the limitless space between spaces, the point between points, the flow within flow. There is nothing that you do not touch and nothing that does not encounter you. You are divine mind, divine body, divine soul. You are the culmination of desire and the seeding of the same. Reach out, and you will find your own self, breathing.

What is your wish for this day? What stirs inside you, hopefully? Will you take a risk toward life? Will you embrace death in all its mystery? They are the same, these two—a cycle, not a continuum—and you are neither, yet you are both. Ah! The Mystery is self. And not self. The Mystery is me. And not me.

And on the æther tolls a mighty bell. The sound rings loud and clear on all the planes. The sound is the tolling of love, the beating of your heart, the shouting of the worlds for justice, the whisper of the secret songs of night.

Each day is new. Each breath another chance. Inhale now, all the way. Hold that air inside you and feel. Exhale all the way. Hold that spaciousness. Now, open! Light appears around you. Is you.

Leap into the void.

Action

1. Sit in silence for ten minutes each day this week. Visualize the still pool and allow your attention to drop into this stillness. Slow your breathing down. Sink. Open. If it helps, count each exhalation, up to ten. Then begin again. Breathe. Be. Sink. Open. Breathe. Be. Sink. Open. Breathe.

2. Go back to the power To Know and bring some of that work into the power To Keep Silence. Can you track a thought process or speech pattern and just breathe with it, allowing it to slow down? What is it trying to tell you? Breathe in to your center and, as you exhale, imagine your breath "pushing" your energy bodies out another two inches around you, giving these things space. Do this with thought or emotion. Then drop the thought or emotion into the pool of stillness in your center. Keep breathing.

3. Notice when you do not want to listen. What can turn this impulse around? What is at the root of this refusal? Is something in you afraid to trust yourself? Is something afraid of the power To Keep Silence? Breathe. Soften. Sink. Just notice. Then sink a little deeper and relax your edges, soft like a gentle rain.

4. What has your mind convinced you that you cannot do? What limits have you placed upon your soul? What structures of practicality have you built around desire? How do you box yourself in? Can you take one further step toward freedom this week? Can you support your practice and desire and help someone else as well? To what activity can you bring the power To Keep Silence? Pick one and try.

CHAPTER 8

YOUR DIVINE WORK IN THE WORLD

In the cave of Destiny, She spins, She weaves, She cuts . . .
FROM MY SONG, "THE FATES"[27]

The more often I enter the cave of stillness, the clearer it becomes that my work has the effect of helping other people truly shine. The work of some of my clients and students may end up having far-reaching consequences heretofore unimagined. They may touch people in ways I can barely comprehend—but I can feel it, and it feels big.

The realization that there are people I know whose work feels this profound fills me with gratitude and gives me a chance to watch the reactions of my ego. Some parts want to set the world on fire with sparks of awareness and creativity. Other parts of my ego just want to live what feels like a simple, ordinary life. And there are yet other parts that say: "Yes! This! My work helps these amazing people!" The latter voices are loudest, but I live somewhere between all of these.

---

27. Available on *Songs for the Waning Year* at *www.sharonknight.bandcamp.com*

My destiny is not to speak to everyone's heart and soul. It is not to make everyone happy. The task undergirding my Divine Work is to return to movement and contemplation every morning, to sit with teachers, and to continue with the practices of self-observation and cleansing—to notice the ways in which I avoid looking at my own reflection, or acting out of fear, or making assumptions. It is never-ending work. It is work that will last a lifetime. It is from all of this that I write, teach, and travel.

Daunting? I could let it become so—and sometimes it feels that way, particularly when I run up against the friction of expectations—but there is also the sense of stillness within and beneath it all. That stillness is what carries me forward. That stillness is what continuously connects me to my destiny. Without it, I think I would be lost.

Whenever my personality gets agitated around the work at hand, there are four options I return to, depending on the duration of the reaction. First, I re-center, I breathe, and I return to stillness, which connects me to compassion. I may ask my personality part what it wants or needs. I may call up a friend to vent for ten minutes. Or I may do a cleansing rite to help me return to balance. No matter which of these I choose, there arises a sense of connection between myself and whatever is upsetting or hurting or irritating me. This sense has been cultivated and is maintained by my consistent return to the cave of stillness. It has taken many years of practice; but, as with all things we practice, it has gotten easier, simpler, and stronger over time.

We want our egos to be our allies, not our slaves or masters. We have success and make mistakes, sometimes moment by moment. We are living in times when many seem to be in great turmoil and forces of upheaval are affecting even the planet: volcanoes, floods, hurricanes, earthquakes, fires, and soaring temperatures. Many spiritual communities are in transition and questioning; countries are at war or are arming for war. In these times, the bedrock of quiet, the opening gates of silence, can be of help.

We are affected as individuals by the forces at work on a global and even cosmic scale. If each individual can remember this and make time to seek out silence, there will be greater equilibrium in our lives, and we can draw from that to help everyone around us more effectively. We can catch our breath and find our way back home.

Soul Support

You mediate the energy of all the worlds. When you live to be cohesive, not scattered or compartmentalized, you become a priest of every moment—in the picking up and the setting down. After the rush from knowledge, to willing, to daring— finally, there is the time of silence and reflection. It is in this that you begin really to notice all the facets of your life and their importance. You pay attention, come to knowledge, and deepen your ability to observe clearly. When you combine will and daring and enter the great silence, you eventually rest upon the shores of your own life and know this: All systems interlock. We are one being.

There is nothing in your life that is outside the purview of your witnessing the sacred. There is no place where you are not shaman, priestess, magic worker, seer of visions large and small. One night, you may dream of floods and wake to the news of tsunami. At work, you may forget that you mediate a larger vision and instead get caught up in the details of your irritation. And yet opportunity always presents itself; you hold your anger and resentment in one hand and your vision for right action in the other. You become the one who rises between them and forms the pillar of your life. But this takes choice. What do you choose? Now. And now. And now.

You can be this pillar for yourself and for others. When our systems interlock, we recognize our oneness with the world. Cairo is not far removed from Madison or Oakland. Japan and New Zealand are sisters of one ocean womb. Fathers feed their children the world over. Wives walk away or stay. Children laugh or cry. And the earth, in some parts poisoned, still gives birth to trees and grasses. Rocks preside, witnessing sunsets.

This earth learns, and we are this earth. And the earth, too, is the cosmos, reaching beyond scattered stars our eyes can never know.

When we commit ourselves to health and wholeness, we commit ourselves to this beloved earth. Everything comes at cost or gift to something else. We eat to fortify ourselves—and for pleasure as well. Then we go out to rebuild that which is broken and to celebrate the love we find along the way.

Commit to silence. Commit to yourself. Commit to the earth. Commit to the sky. Commit to above and to below. Commit to the ocean and the tiny fronds of ferns on distant islands. We are separate, it is true; but together, we remember to be whole.

What rituals will be your teachers? Choose these.

ON STOPPING

To create, we need space to do so, often in the form of silence and time.

NILOFER MERCHANT

The power To Keep Silence leads us toward greater depth, flexibility, and strength. Including it in our practice is vital for our health, and for the continuance of our Divine Work in the world. When we ignore it, we suffer. Moreover, our work suffers, and we feed the over-culture that tells us that slowing down is for the weak. They tell us we can have it all, and that we can do anything if we just try hard enough. Sometimes, however, we try too hard—and then we crash.

This is a strong reminder that we need space and time, and that the cultivation of inner quiet is necessary not only for our creative process, but for our health. To Keep Silence includes the ability to pause. This pause carries the lessons of the hushed hours after midnight, of the stillness of dark winter, and of the soul resting deeply, seeking renewal. Sometimes we need to stop doing in order to open to our Being.

We cannot create the life that we desire if there is no room for silence.

A STORY ABOUT STOPPING

I was on airplanes nine times in three months, including teaching trips to England, Germany, Canada, and the Mid-Atlantic coast. Between trips, I taught classes in my local area, saw clients, worked on this book, launched a video teaching series, launched an e-publishing venture, kept up with my dedicated students, dealt with some necessary fires, took an unemployed family member into my home, and started an online class.[28]

This came hard on the heels of a few years of intense work, including other very similar periods of overwork. That spring, I hit a wall. I said, literally, "I'm finished," and took to my bed for a day. But I still had many teaching trips on the books, along with all the other work that I had said I would do. For years, I knew I needed to cut back on travel, yet I allowed my travel to increase. After all, these were teaching trips, and teaching is what I love to do. But I knew the structure of how I worked needed to change. I was not heeding the power To Keep Silence. I was not remembering the need for gestation. My life was not set up to nurture any seeds.

Because I am a person who responds well to discipline, I got by for awhile. But by summer, the sheer number of things I had set myself toward and the energy required to make them happen were just too many and too much. I was suffering from what I've heard called "capacity overestimation."[29] So I increased my exercise routine and further cleaned up my diet to gather the energetic resources required. I kept up meditation and prayers. However, I started skipping my full days off. I counted working a few hours in the morning and then doing something else as a day off. I started working early and late. I cut back on the things that fed my creativity, and yet wondered why I was having such trouble getting this book into a shape that worked.

I wasn't taking my own advice. I was pushing too hard. I convinced myself that the problems I was encountering were all

---

28. The video teaching series is "Fiat LVX!" and the publishing ventures are Lvx/Nox and Sunna Press. Information is available *at www.thorncoyle.com*.

29. I heard this from Isabel Partlett, quoting Lissa Boles—both life coaches.

problems of privilege anyway—that I have a great life and didn't really have anything to complain about. I'd announced these various projects and promised things to people, so they had to get done. That was all true. But that doesn't mean it was working. As a matter of fact, it is something of a miracle that as much got accomplished as did, considering I was running at a deficit. I knew all this, and was still trying to be diligent, so I *did* try to slow down. I switched from lifting weights to yoga, allowed my spiritual practice to tune toward listening, and took more half days off. Finally, I said to myself that I would only do the work directly in front of me, and let the larger projects lie fallow for awhile.

It was too late, however. The thing I always tell people will happen, did happen—I crashed. I took to bed on a Friday after a morning yoga class at the ashram near my home. Saturday morning, I was scheduled to lead a workshop at a conference. I got up and talked to one of my partners about whether or not we would go out to breakfast. I said: "It isn't the going out to breakfast that feels hard; it is the bathing, getting dressed, and then going to breakfast that feels hard." He looked at me and replied: "If you are too sick to go to breakfast, you are too sick to teach." I did what I hate most—I canceled my presentation and went to bed. The incipient vertigo, wooziness, mild fever, and exhaustion all added up to a virus and overextension. Forced by circumstance and wise words from a friend, I finally took my own advice.

I preach integration and bringing all our parts to our Divine Work. After years of developing will and discipline, I needed to learn how to include the parts that need deep rest, that need more downtime so creativity can flourish, that need more laughter and time with friends.

When we feel as if we are crashing, it is time to pause and gather energy, because a big shift we cannot quite see around the corner is likely coming. And even if it isn't, we'll be healthier in the long run if we get some rest.

Soul Support

The well of silence welcomes you.

Allow yourself to listen. Allow yourself to sink. To float. To rest. To open.

Silence empties you of hurry. Silence fills you with a ringing presence beyond the mind. It includes everything. Silence carries you, in stillness, ever deeper.

The practice of listening and allowing silence to grow within your field makes you stronger, clearer, and more potent. Give up your bustle and worry for five minutes. Then ten. Then twenty. Over time, the silence will infuse even your laughter, adding a rich, bass note to your life. You will be whole, not a walking set of fragments glued together by your thoughts or your emotions. Silence, deep silence, connects you to yourself. Palpable. Gorgeous. Open to this green earth, the coming new moon, and the mysteries of the stars.

The more you cultivate spiritual silence, the clearer your sense of justice will be, and the more powerful your actions and your words. Do not be silent for silence's sake. Rather, let the well of silence teach you the power of all sound. Sink onto the bench, or the prayer rug. Light the candles on your altar. Settle your attention in your belly. Let the tip of your tongue rise up to meet your palate. Close your eyes and breathe.

GIVING WAY TO SILENCE

In Part I of this book, we discussed the power of stories and how grappling with them helps us toward knowledge. I would like to speak now of the ways in which stories must give way to silence.

Some challenges grind us down. Others help focus our will and clarify our lives and our intentions. We can assess the difference by noticing our energy levels in both the short and longer term. Are you numb with exhaustion, or do you feel tired in a healthy, satisfied way? Do you dread facing your projects or notice that, even when resistance is present, there is another part of you that feels engaged and interested? This sort of noticing is helped by cultivating silence.

When we open ourselves to the stillness and silence inside for long enough, we begin to recognize which voice is that of an ego trapped in stories, and which is the part of our selves that wishes to move forward anyway, despite the odds, the struggle, the sense of shame, hubris, anger, or self-righteousness. We balance these facets of ego and come to what is important: our growth as humans and our contribution to the world.

Our Sufi brothers and sisters tell us to "Die before you die." They are speaking of dying to the parts of ego that keep us sequestered from mystery—that are noisily objecting or clinging in apathy or shame. These are the parts of self that most fear change. Yet these are the very parts that need change the most. We don't have to get rid of these facets of ego, but we can bring them toward greater health and harmony with our deeper purpose. We can die to their control and help them to be reborn in a more useful manner. We can change.

If we don't return to silence, the task of changing is almost impossible. We must cultivate stillness inside to have a healthy place from which to assess the wants, needs, and desires of ego, and to get these on board the larger projects of our souls. Unless we do this daily, when push comes to shove, all we have to help us are teachings from the over-culture about getting ahead or voices from the past that keep us down.

If we don't meet each day from a pool of silence, we will drown in the noise of our own making. The clamor of the over-culture will hijack our best intentions over and over. Our egos will never learn to be the strong allies they need to be for us to manifest the life we most deeply desire, the life that will be of help to the world.

The next time you find yourself caught in a story—repeating to friends, colleagues, or your journal why you can't do this thing, how you've been wronged, why you are right, or what pattern keeps you back—take a moment and answer the invitation given on each breath: come to life, to spaciousness, and to silence. Breath helps our frustrated and bewildered parts of self to meet silence again, to pause naturally and with grace. When silence meets anything else, myriad possibilities open, giving us insight and opportunity that were not available when all we could do was rail against the cages we perceived.

Stillness brings the ego back toward balance, love, and power. When we bring the ego into stillness, we can see and hear so much more, which gets us closer to the underlying truth of each situation, and of our lives as a whole.

I repeat: This is not the silence of suppression that leads to oppression. This is the still silence of the self attempting something new—to live centered around a still pool at our core, in order to cultivate true autonomy and choice. This stillness is the seat of real power. With it, over time, we can do almost anything. It also helps to clarify desire, allowing us to recognize on a deep level that we are walking the path of the soul.

Breath moves and pauses, moves and pauses. We inhale. Pause. We exhale. Pause. The pauses are natural rests occurring between the giving out and taking in of air. The earth of the body is the container for this flow.

Soul Support

Here is a brief meditation to help you slow down inside and return to the breath of life.

Tune out distractions and dive into the still pool of your soul. Compassion. Fatigue. Worry. Feelings of being overwhelmed. Let them drop for now. Imagine yourself in a pool, a pond, or a still bay. Let yourself float in the warm waters of renewal. There is nothing happening that you can solve by pacing the floor, or lying awake, or resisting, or propping up. Float awhile. Breathe deeply, from the soles of your feet to the crown of your head. Allow life to enter your cells again, one by one.

Still floating, breathe in slowly, and then hold that air inside. Allow oxygen to replace the toxins built up by stress, weariness, fear, or over-functioning. Exhale slowly, and then open up again to breath. Cycle. Circulate. Just be. Do this for as long as you need to; float in this cradling pool for as long as feels right. Drift a little. Breathe. When you feel ready, open your eyes. Drink some water. Stretch your limbs and smile.

Now get up again, and return to those things that give you strength and meaning. Engage with the tasks at hand.

To do your best work requires renewal. Take five minutes, half an hour, half a day.

The world will still be waiting.

Action

1. This week, find a way to offer rest to the parts of yourself that may feel agitated or be in pain. Go for a walk. Relax in a bath. Just breathe with those parts.

2. What parts of yourself have you been avoiding? What is the advice you need to take? How will you help yourself, so you can better help the world? Reexamine your To Do list. Is there one thing you can remove from it? Better yet, work on a Stop Doing list.[30]

3. Every day, practice centering in stillness and expanding your energy bodies in order to make space. You can find descriptions of these in the Soul Support portions of chapters 0 and 1.

4. What in you needs rest or contemplation? Make space for these parts. Take time off. Increase your meditation or contemplation practices. Do some spiritual reading. Listen to music. Take a walk in a beautiful place—under trees, in the desert, on a shore.

---

30. The "Stop Doing List" is a business concept pioneered by Jim Collins (see *www.jimcollins.com*). I heard about it from Padma Maxwell *www.padmamaxwell.com*.

TRANSITION

THE RITUAL
OF SILENCE

. . . it is necessary to KEEP SILENT with discernment.

ELIPHAS LÉVI

Once again, do whatever helps alert your soul that you are enter-ing a different space and time than is ordinary for you. You may wish to sit or stand at an altar, or go to a favorite place outside. Just make sure you have twenty to thirty minutes of privacy. Have a journal on hand to make any notes when you return. A cup of wa-ter is also helpful to drink at the end, to bring yourself fully back into the present. For this ritual, you may wish to have a favorite stone to hold, although you can just imagine one.

Imagine you can travel to your place of power, your sacred place—the grove of your heart, the cave of your soul, the temple of your mind. Relax into your body. Take five deep breaths. Let each exhalation be another step toward your sacred place. Imagine yourself entering. What does it look like? Are there trees, ani-mals, columns, glass, brick, desert vistas, or a night sky? Is there the scent of plants or of rain on stones? Is there incense burning, snaking upward? Do ravens call or bells ring? Just notice. This is your space.

Settle in. Open to your breath. Feel the solidity of your body, and the structure of your bones. Drop into the stillness at your core. As you breathe, begin to imagine that this stillness can expand outward, becoming larger. Let your whole body, and then your whole being, be filled with this sense of stillness. Relax. Hold a stone in your hands. Feel the weight of it, the silence of it. Imagine the mystery it holds, collected over the course of hundreds or thousands of years. Feel that sense of mystery expanding into your own stillness. What do you hold inside you, as you hold this stone? Connect to the earth upon which you stand or sit. Notice how gravity draws you toward the very earth that supports you. Let yourself sit. Just be for a moment. Allow time and space to stretch around you.

When you are ready, speak from the place of stillness at your core: "I expand in the power To Keep Silence. I hold the mystery. I am one with the gestation of desire." Feel the silence permeating the structure of your body and your soul.

Stay here. Be still. Breathe.

When it feels like time to return, thank this place, this time. Bow deeply. Then on five long breaths, come back to ordinary space and time. Take a breath from the soles of your feet to the crown of your head. Feel the strength of your bones and the silence at your center. Blessed be the power To Keep Silence.

Drink some water. Write. Rest. Be.

INVOKING THE NEXT POWER

Remember your breath and how the great pause leads once again to movement. Inhale. Pause. Now exhale. The power To Keep

Silence has renewed you, and will continue to open you to the greater Mystery. You carry more presence and greater connection to your Being and its relationship to the cosmos.

With time as your ally, you can now move toward the power To Manifest. You can manifest your heart's desire and enact your purpose in the world. Those who are still exploring what this means will have a chance to take the actions needed to deepen their quest. Wherever you are in your relationship to purpose and desire, you can change yourself, in order to better change this world.

PART V
To Manifest

WE ASK THE WISE COUNCIL:

How do you approach risk?

I risk every day by going into some of the most challenging of areas and working with some of the most challenging circumstances. I don't just risk safety, although that is present at times, but I risk a broken heart. I watch some of the most incredible kids who are shot down by guns and sacrificed by the system, leaving me scared for them and with the heaviest of hearts. Yet I know that these connections and experiences also feed my spiritual soul by allowing me to do the work of the Gods and teaching me how to live for today and love for this moment. I approach risk by allowing myself to be of service and trusting that I will receive abundance by sharing abundance with others.

CRYSTAL BLANTON

I have always taken risks because when you see something for yourself, it is not always true that others see it as well. When I was seventeen, I was offered a full scholarship to study piano at the University of Florida in Gainesville. I was going to start winter term and about two weeks before I was slotted to attend, the professor called me up and told me he didn't have the proper paperwork for me to come down. I told him, I already quit my job and was planning to come there. I told him, I would come anyways and see what happens. For me, the worst case scenario would be that I spent two weeks in Florida (on vacation) and then flew back to Toronto, Canada. When I got there, I didn't know where I would stay, nothing. I didn't care. I knew it would work out somehow. I met with the chair of the music department and the professor who invited me to the school and they made a "special" visa happen for me for the first term. I stayed in Florida that winter and studied piano.

DANA REASON

By going to the darkest corners of my psyche and revealing (without judgment) the most hidden parts of me to myself and giving them some sort of voice. That way, I can learn what those hidden motivations have to offer and perhaps take some of the charge off of them. This is awkward! Laughing as much as I can, outing it and telling others about it. Taking the pressure off of needing to be deep, meaningful, and significant all the time. Embracing the lightness and small talk once in awhile.

SUZANNE STERLING

CHAPTER 9
THE QUINTESSENCE

I have gone beyond vision into many of the experiences described in Eastern and Western literature—the transcendence of the subject-object relationship, the sense of solidarity with all the world so that one actually knows by experience what "God is love" means; the sense that, in spite of death and suffering, everything is somehow ultimately All Right; the sense of boundless gratitude at being privileged to inhabit this universe. Blake says, "Gratitude is heaven itself"—it used to be an incomprehensible phrase, now I know precisely what he was talking about.

ALDOUS HUXLEY[31]

We are not at the end. Not by a long shot. Where we are on the journey is a harmonizing place often known as the "quintessence"—the fifth element from which all others emerge and into

---

31. From *Moksha*, Michael Horowitz and Cynthia Palmer, eds. (Park Street Press, 1977). This is a collection of Huxley's writings on his experiences with psychedelics. While I am not a user of psychedelics myself, his descriptions bring to mind spiritual and mystical experiences that I and others have encountered on the way.

which they all pour. When we recognize that seeking knowledge, building will, taking risks, and sinking into silence are all infused with the same substance, everything in our lives comes together. Something changes.

This is not a change propped up by activity or simple habit. This is a change that touches our very essence, because our lives have gotten a glimpse or a taste of the essence of the world. God Hirself has touched us, fully, even if only for an instant. Our hearts respond to this touch and radiate wholeness through our being. Our multiple facets no longer fight so hard with one another, but act in concert. We reflect the wholeness of the cosmos at its best.

Whether this happens for five minutes, five hours, five days, or five years is immaterial. What matters is that something in us has shifted toward integration, and all of our parts can work together in the flow of destiny. Activation leads to manifestation, which leads us deeper into our lives' purpose. We begin to live more easily, more surely, and more openly.

REMAINING ENGAGED

When I went back to school in my thirties, I had a geology class with a professor who was not very skilled at making the material interesting. In other words, he was practically sleep-inducing. I figured out a strategy to keep myself interested. When one of the other students was complaining about the boring course, I told him my secret, which probably failed to impress him: "I just try to learn one new thing every day." That helped me a lot during that class. It reminded me of why I was there in the first place, and kept me engaged in the process when other parts of me just wanted to shut down. Had I allowed myself to tune out during that class, I would have learned nothing at all. Now, I can't say that I retained much from the course material itself, but I learned something very important, nonetheless: My engagement is up to me, not anything outside of me.

We can choose to be interested rather than waiting for something to strike our fancy. We can choose to become engaged. Choosing engagement puts us in the power position, over and over. We get a chance to invoke all four Powers of the Sphinx and show up for ourselves, despite mediocre professors, cranky coworkers, subpar equipment, allergies, emotional upheaval, or anything else that may come our way.

A STORY ABOUT ENGAGEMENT

After getting my ass kicked at the gym one day, I was in the locker room with a woman who used to lift at a grotty working-class gym in the Mission District of San Francisco, as I did when I was still dancing semiprofessionally.[32] The neighborhood has been gentrified, and that gym no longer exists. She has gone on to become a full-time trainer, while I have drifted in and out of various forms of exercise before finding myself back in yet another locker room.

Glancing at her broad back, I remarked: "I thought you were big twenty years ago; you are even bigger now!" She replied that she had goals to reach, so that was the general plan, and that she, at the very least, tried to maintain. Then she said something interesting: "Even when you're just going for maintenance, progress ends up getting made." I remarked that this seemed true for any practice.

---

32. I danced with FatChanceBellydance under the direction of founder Carolena Nericcio in the late 1980s through the mid-1990s. Before "Tribal Style Bellydance" took off, we were rehearsing in the back of a San Francisco church and performing at tattoo events (see *www.fcbd.com*).

I pondered this while riding my bike to my next appointment. Why is this true of so many things? Physical health, meditation, writing, dance, job skills, etc. What is it about maintenance that ends up facilitating growth? The answer seems to be commitment. For all of these things, we make a commitment to ourselves and to our projects. We state that something is important enough for effort. And even if we aren't going full-out, we still end up building muscle, so to speak. We end up learning something. We show up to ourselves and for ourselves.

REMAINING COMMITTED

Commitment may not start every single thing, but it starts the flow toward *manifestation*. Commitment ignites the action of the will. It takes what may be a small impulse, even a daydream, and makes the first step toward channeling it into action. Commitment is the goad to the spirit, the cheerleader, and the stalwart support. Commitment is the thing that keeps us showing up.

Derek Sivers asks: "What do you hate not doing?" Let us look at that a bit. What can you not avoid anymore? What engages you regardless of what your mind may tell you is prudent? What do you do even when other people think it is silly or you worry that it is too hard? What gives you a secret thrill? What happens when you choose boldness and say to your spirit: "I commit to this"?

Remember, sometimes showing up is half the battle; at other times, showing up is what gets things started.

Despite everything I just wrote, some days we still wake up and don't want to do what is required to manifest our Divine Work in the world. On those days, I find that doing the smallest thing that connects me to that work can be of help. Yes, that can often open up the flow of energy. More important, however, it reminds me that connecting to my soul is important. Making even small efforts—although on some days, for some people, they can feel huge—reminds me that my life matters.

A Story about Commitment

Chandra was having a much-needed meltdown one day. Out of her mouth came these words: "If I do all this spiritual work and I'm still not getting what I want, why bother?" My first response was that she mattered, her life mattered, her thread in the web of life mattered. We then went on to look at how something she thought of as a truth was just another story based on fear. Her soul was heading in the right direction, but parts of her personality were still holding back. Recognizing this, she was able to go another layer deeper and a step farther toward manifesting her desire.

In moving toward activation, don't forget that it requires all of the other powers, including making space for silence. In working to manifest desire, remember compassion.

MANAGING DISAPPOINTMENT

One thing that can get in the way of commitment and manifestation of desire is fear of disappointment. In me, this has looked like not wanting to disappoint myself or others by giving up early instead of giving something my all. For instance, practicing flashcard drills with my father was a quick way to shut me out of math, because, if I didn't immediately know the answer, he shouted at me. Disappointment turned too quickly to punishment, frightening me. This caused me to stick to the things at which I felt more naturally skilled. I've had to work to allow myself to be "bad" at things so that I can actually keep learning.

A Story about Disappointment

Charles is a powerful and conscientious man who was continuously getting stuck when he reached a certain point in relationships and in growing his business. He had been doing a lot of work on noticing the patterns at play energetically, emotionally, and physically. During one appointment, it finally came out that he had grown used to not asking for things so that he would not be disappointed. This had entered his life during his preteen to early teen years when he figured out that he couldn't rely on his mother for follow-through. The disappointment wounded him so much that he just stopped asking.

During the time we worked together, Charles was actively putting in the effort to grow his small business and doing all the right things—working with clarifying intention, applying will to right actions, studying business theory, offering free lectures, doing spiritual cleansing, and working some manifestation magic. Things still weren't moving the way he thought they should, even when he took an economic downturn into consideration.

We finally uncovered a fear of disappointment. I could see something open in him after he spoke these words to me: "I am afraid that, if I ask for what I want or need, I will be disappointed again." Speaking the words out loud was the next step he needed to take toward manifesting his desire. Charles had invoked the power To Know, which made his further work with the powers To Will and To Dare more effective and potent.

Charles's predicament is a perfect example of how we need to cycle through the Four Powers at different phases in our lives. He had been working diligently on all of the powers, including the fifth, but had not included a very important piece of himself in the process. Once he began the work of welcoming that disappointed part home, what he desired—to grow his business of helping people heal—had a far better chance of coming to fruition.

Soul Support

What are you still excluding? Do you need to do another round of calling your soul back from its hiding places? Sometimes you can do this by noticing what still feels as if it were missing. At other times, you need to invite the nonverbal to crack open your subconscious more fully so you can see, hear, or feel something to which you usually don't have access.

Gather together collage materials. Save catalogs, beg old calendars or magazines from friends, and plunder the cards you have been sent. Get a good-size piece of heavy paper or poster board. It can help to pick a colored piece of paper so you don't become intimidated by an expanse of white. Get a glue stick and some scissors.

Once you have gathered your materials, allow yourself thirty minutes to work on this project. You can go for longer if you wish, but it is helpful to your emotional soul to have a clear boundary and container. Breathe and find your center and circumference. Call upon support from earth and sky. Then ask your soul these questions:

- Will you please uncover for me that which will help me to move forward, to heal, to manifest my Divine Work?

- Will you please show what is hidden in me?

• Will you bring that which was obscured to light?

Go for thirty minutes, picking out images that appeal, not worrying about what they are. Go for color, form, or how they make you feel. Once you have a good pile gathered, begin to rip or cut them into shapes that resonate. Tear away what isn't needed, leaving what moves you. Then start to arrange them on the paper. Don't glue yet. Once the placement feels right, begin to glue from the bottom layers up. Sometimes the collage will change at this point. Let it. Stay with your intuition. Once you feel complete for now, step back.

Look. What do you see?

DEEPER CHOICES

We cannot cure the world of sorrows, but we can choose to live in joy.

JOSEPH CAMPBELL

In Part II, we looked at the importance of choosing willingly. When it comes time to manifest our Divine Work in the world, to activate our true purpose, we naturally begin looking at deeper choices.

We sometimes talk about this as putting down the urgent to take up the important. In order to manifest our larger desires—the Work of This God that comes from our best selves—we must find ways to shift our patterns of urgency. Some, conversely, need to shift their patterns of sloth or apathy. Working through the Four Powers helps with this, and we can move through the cycle multiple times in our lives. Each time, we will be well served by restating our intentions and attempting to connect with the deeper desire of our souls.

What is your purpose? Some may still not have a clear answer to this. To them, I say: "Your work right now is to engage consistently with your heart and soul, to show up for practice, and to learn to listen to the cosmos." A clear sense of purpose is served by the same things. For me to manifest my mandate—To Teach—I must continue to engage, practice, and listen. I've gotten caught in the smaller cycles myself, thinking I was best serving my larger purpose. In order to tap deeper and broader streams of connection to my work, however, I sometimes have to take several steps back, to slow down again, and to deepen my listening practice. Only then can there be space for a yet deeper layer to emerge that enables me see that even my Divine Work may be deeper than I know. For example, as my work continues, I am coming to see that underpinning the mandate To Teach is the mandate To Love. The manifestation of our purpose is a process just like any other, filled with arcs both large and small.

We all have the task of looking at the very long arc to see how that is braided with our connection to God Hirself, to flow, to the cosmos. We can then look at the arc of the year. And only then can we look at the smaller arcs of activity in our lives. All of these need to support each other for us to manifest the life for which we are destined.

Two Stories about Choices

Rhonda was struggling with getting caught, over and over, in cycles that burned her out and interrupted her sleep. Sleep-deprived, she ended up unbalanced and off center. I reminded her of the intention she had to a larger arc of being and practice. Her commitment to the work her soul longed for was not being served by her constant caretaking of others and her putting out of a series of metaphorical fires. She was living too much with the sorrows of the world and too little with the joy.

Jasper is a man of honor who values service and leadership. This can mean he takes on too much responsibility, not leaving enough room for his own needs to be met or for others to step forward into success or failure. He carries a strong warrior archetype and does his soul's work well, but sometimes the man beneath the archetype feels lonely. He, too, is learning to practice paying greater attention to the large arc of service rather than the small emergencies that cross his path on a regular basis. Consequently, work and friendships feel more nourishing and exciting, and he has allowed himself to fall in love.

DESIRE AND OTHERS

Question: Is part of adulthood putting aside desire for the sake of duty?

Balancing our wants and desires with the needs of those closest to us can feel like walking a tightrope, even when our purpose is clear, let alone when we are still feeling our way forward. In those cases, we need to have honest conversations with ourselves and our close loved ones about risk assessment, desire, and what we all really want. We need to do some of the work To Dare in order to manifest the life of our choosing, the life we are meant to lead.

When we feel trapped, we can't help anyone. Our life energy becomes constricted and manifesting something healthy becomes impossible. If we feel trapped, we need to find ways to alter our condition or perhaps shift our attitudes and energy to get things flowing again. Sometimes there are options we have not looked at because we get so used to seeing things in a certain way. And sometimes we need to reframe our desires.

Are there ways to shift things around in your current situation to get some of what you want, need, and desire? Can some of the changes come in other ways, starting from inside? Desire is deep and abiding; it harnesses life force. It isn't about running from problems or living in "castles in the sky." Desire is something true in your soul that just won't quit.

My soul's purpose has led me through many life phases and even caused the breakup of long-term relationships that grew too constricting, despite my attempts to hold on to them, to fix them, to do my best. I *did* do my best, and they still crumbled. It felt wrenching, heartbreaking, and horrible. My heart and soul needed to move on anyway.

I believe that, because I was following this calling of my heart and soul rather than running from conflict or seeking an easy cure, I have been able to build new things from the sturdy foundation of practice and commitment. These things stand now and grow, feeding and supporting my life.

I've seen this over and over with friends, students, and clients. Sometimes life circumstances like jobs or relationships weather the changes, becoming richer and stronger in the process, with all parties served by the expansion and the deeper truths being told and then lived. In other cases, things that were weaker or brittler cracked at the influx of the pure energy of change. In all these cases, because the people in question were sincerely trying to live closer to integrity and follow their hearts' desires, life worked out well. This can take time. But it is time well worth investing.

Duty and desire need not be at odds with one another. We may need to reassess whether what we are naming as desire is really something we think we want, without the underlying current of need. It may be that we are trying to escape a deeper wish that may feel more frightening: deeper intimacy, more responsibility, a simpler life, greater exposure, or expansion of self. One person asked me whether her wish to move across the country was at odds with what was best for her family. I asked: "What in you wants the move? What do you think will change in your life? What do you want that you do not currently have?" Whatever our worries are, our duty must be to serve our souls' desire. To do anything less is to leave unclaimed the work that only we can do. Pretty soon, everything else becomes a half-truth, and our lives become half-lived.

Soul Support

When you feel at a crossroads, you are well served by walking yourself back through the Four Powers. What does your mind say you want? Breathe into it. Walk it through the power To Know. Ask desire some questions. Imagine yourself fulfilled. Then move on to the power To Will. What is required of you to really commit to the life you are building, to your Divine Work in the world? Are you willing to make the changes required? Next, step into the power To Dare. Does this feel like a risk worth taking? Is there energy for that risk, even if some of the fuel comes from fear?

Now sit in the power To Keep Silence. Hold your desire. Breathe. What does it feel like now? What is the next step that will take you toward activation and manifestation? What in you—emanating from your core outward—brings the Four Powers together in order to enter the flow of your destiny?

And does your destiny feel like this thing you said you desire? If not, are you willing to release it and recommit to the process your heart and soul deserve?

THE IMPORTANCE OF FAILURE

The only undefeated fighters never fought. Victory comes from loss. While voices may chide you for the supposed hubris of your dreams, the gratification of a life lived with triumphs favors those bold enough to get knocked down and out. None of us gets out of here alive, so accept that it'll be messy and painful, get back up and go kick ass anyway. Quitting or never trying are the only real defeats.

SCOTT SONNON[33]

We've already talked about the importance of learning from failure, but I want to revisit it as we examine manifestation.

I fail every day. Just ask my students. I also succeed. The same students—or clients, or friends—will likely tell you that as well. My work is to teach, to mentor, to write, to present, and to show up. My work is also to answer emails in a timely fashion, to keep on top of the projects I begin, to remain accountable to volunteers, to practice and study, and to spend time with my friends, partners, and beloveds. My work is to listen, to plan, to remain open to what is around me, and to set boundaries when appropriate. My work is to get things done. My work is to learn.

---

33. Master Coach and martial artist. You can find his work at *www.scottsonnon.com.*

If I fail at these things each day, why do I keep working? Why do I start new projects? Let me explain something: My brain leaps from square one to square four. It's the way I'm wired. In trying to hold this in check, I can temper the impulse to *go-go-go* and to *start-start-start*. But sometimes it gets the better of me. I see the vision so clearly, or I've been holding off for five years on these projects I've been guided to spearhead, or the stated needs of clients or others have been loud enough, for long enough, that I acquiesce.

This is a good thing about me; it means that I am following the call of spirit. But this very thing also proves to be problematic. I trip and fall sometimes and paint too grand a vision too far in advance. Projects get delayed for myriad reasons. Responses get buried at the bottom of the To Do list.

Yet, in the midst of all of this fumbling, a lot gets done. If I never overshot myself, manifestation might still be relegated to the realm of dreams and wishes. Instead, hardy fool that I am, I take the dare and leap.

In thinking about pursuing our desires, it can be helpful to assess—likely for the hundredth time—how we feel about failure and success. If thoughts of either collapse us or send us running for the nearest hermitage, we must ask ourselves why. What is the resistance that still runs our lives?

To activate the Four Powers of the Sphinx and manifest purpose require that we let go of our ideas of success and failure. Manifestation lives in the active place of opening, following, and knowing when and where to steer. To activate is to set things in motion. To do this, we need everything that has come before; every scrap of the fabric of our lives must be sewn into this. Nothing can hide from the fulfillment of our souls' desire. Anything in our blind spots, or things we are avoiding, will still form the shape of our failure and success.

This is what I mean by assessing our relationship to success and failure. We need a deeper reassessment when we are in the phase of manifestation. I have to know my tendencies. Sometimes these undermine my projects, and sometimes they goad me toward success. My deepest failings are often the very things that fuel my life's work. They keep me human and whole, and help me act as though—like Prometheus—I can steal fire from the Gods.

Working magic means showing up with our demons and our divinity, our sorrow and our joy. Alchemy only happens when we are willing to go through the processes of gathering together, refining, pouring, and solidifying. In the end, we have something fine to hold.

Can you think of failure and success as necessary ingredients to the magical creation that flows from the alembic of desire? Accepting yourself in this radical way enables you to act freely in the world, bringing forth your Divine Work—in cocreation with the cosmos and reunited with God Hirself.

UNDERESTIMATING SUCCESS

Success can be subtle; it sometimes masquerades as ordinary life.

By not settling for "good enough," by following desire and applying will and intention to practice, by observing ourselves and our habits over time, we know ourselves better. Shifts occur. All of a sudden, we are not lost for days in emotional cycles or mental arguments. We say we will do something and we follow through. More changes happen. We notice more. In this noticing, sometimes we fail to notice the biggest thing of all: we have had many successes. What we wished to ignite within ourselves now burns with a steady fire. We no longer need as many spells and prayers to ask for what we want, because we have increased our capability to manifest desire through our sheer presence. We are living more integrated lives.

Sure, there is always another challenge around the corner. Certainly, there are still personality parts we have to live with, for good or for ill. But I like to remind myself that this is how we learn. We once struggled to learn to read and write the simplest things. Now we most often take this incredible skill for granted. It is the same with spiritual practice and other life successes. Everything follows patterns of growth, plateau, and decay. We can pick up something new as some other thing loses energy. We can keep revitalizing our relationship with every facet of our lives. The opportunity here is endless—particularly for those privileged enough to have their basic physical needs met.

Fortune is found where grace meets effort. In the power To Manifest, we combine knowing, willing, daring, and the fertile space of silence. The eagle, the lion, the human, and the bull all work together, becoming strong and lively within us, forming the Sphinx and allowing magic to happen. Something stirs in sex, belly, heart, or mind. This becomes a warmth, a heat, a passion that radiates out from our core, infusing the rest of our being. It even illuminates our fear.

Fear teaches us. Fear shows us our resistance. Fear can protect us, and fear can hold us back. We can look at our current conversations with fear and with inspiration. We do need inspiration—that is food for our desire. Most mornings over tea and oatmeal, I do some spiritual or inspirational reading. Whereas meditation and exercise build a container for my work, this reading is one of the things that refill the water skin. It quenches my thirst, enabling me to move again, activating my vision and my will—and sometimes it reminds me why I'm on this quest in the first place.

Soul Support

How often are you present to your practice, your family, and your desire? What feels as if it is working? What works so well now that you barely notice it? Remember how it used to seem like an obstacle? Even if things feel really difficult today—physically, spiritually, financially, emotionally—can you center and breathe long enough to notice how far you've come in even one area of your life? Generally, in times of difficulty, at least one of what I call "The Planes of Stability" is in a state of balance and blessing.[34] Go through these planes now: spiritual practice, home and relationships, physical health, mental and emotional health, money and work, relationship to Nature. What is working? What gives a sense of satisfaction? What feels like a blessing? Into what have you put effort? What is in a different place now than it was five years ago as a result of that will and intention?

BECOMING YOUR OWN MENTOR

If you're comfortable, cool and clear-sighted, then the shade you're standing in most likely is being cast from someone else's shadow. If you're feeling uncomfortable, hot and uncertain,

---

34. More information on working with the Planes of Stability can be found in my book *Kissing the Limitless* (Weiser Books, 2009).

you're probably the one casting the shadow. Turn towards the source of your discomfort and stand on your own. Shine your own light.

Scott Sonnon

What kind of person would you like to be? Honest and strong? Generous? Skilled and disciplined? Dedicated? Lighthearted? We often look outside ourselves for inspiration, and that can be very helpful. I have a roster of "usual suspects"—friends, writers, teachers, and philosophers—to whom I turn for doses of insight. This helps me with perspective, gets my brain turning, and activates my soul. What sustains me, however, must come from within. Otherwise, too much looking for inspiration outside can cause me to compare myself to others too much. We each have our own work, our own desires, and our own places in the cosmos. We cannot simply pattern ourselves on others—and certainly not after we have reached adulthood.

The only person you are competing with is yourself, and it is a competition to live the life you desire as the person you wish to be. Do you wish to be clearheaded and centered when faced with adversity? Practice. Do you wish to be a person so dedicated that you get up early before work to write short stories, exercise, or pray? Set the alarm and pay attention. Begin to model the very behavior you wish to emulate and, in so doing, you begin to model the life you wish to live.

I show up to the mat, the meditation bench, and the computer keyboard because that is the person I wish to be. I adjust my attitude when I'm feeling fractious, because I want to remember that my problems or irritations are those that stem from relative privilege. And that's the person I wish to be. I want to model my best behavior whenever possible, as a reminder that this behavior is helpful to my long-term goals while other behaviors undermine my efforts. This isn't Pollyanna talk; it actually makes good sense. If you are to become the person you wish to be, you have to act accordingly. This isn't "Fake it 'til you make it" either. Adopting this pattern says, rather: "I have the ability within myself *right now* to follow through on my stated intentions, to support my dreams, and to act with greater generosity and compassion." Begin where you are, honestly assessing your strengths and weaknesses. Choose to stop undermining yourself. One step at a time, choose to stop selling yourself short.

Scott Sonnon, whose quote leads off this section, comes from a background of great adversity—poor, with learning disabilities, in bad physical health, and briefly relegated to a mental institution, as were scores of misfit teens in the 1980s. Unsupported by parents or teachers and beaten up by peers, he figured out who he wanted to be inside and has worked his whole life to get there. He's a strong man, a healthy man, a spiritual man, a parent, and an apparent success. Having no immediate good role models, he became one for himself.

Times may feel hard, but inside of us there is an amazing force. We have to choose to seek it out, to bolster it, bit by bit, and to follow its lead. What job we have doesn't matter. Where we live is of little consequence. Some have it easier in social or economic terms, but all have the spark of desire inside. Once we free ourselves from needing our lives to look like someone else's, we can become our own role models. Therein lies power.

Soul Support

How do you respond when you feel you are not at your best, have not given your full effort, have been less than graceful or clear? What is your wish then? Do you still have a wish to know? Does anger or shame rise up inside you?

You walk the path that is your own and that path winds along with other roads, forming a pattern of life. You walk the path in beauty, at one with trees and stones and houses and animals. You walk the path and stumble. You walk in brightest sunshine and deepest midnight, with only the stars as your guides. Sometimes you walk when the sky is clouded over, and you fear you have lost your way.

But still, there is the path. Still, your feet find their way again, even when it seems you've taken some ancillary road, some diversion or digression, paused to rest, or even fallen down.

Bring it all to the seeking. Bring it all to the moving. Bring it all to the sitting still. There is nothing you cannot bring to your awakening. There is nothing that is not the flow of life. The secret is remembering. The secret is choosing to bring it all, not to hide. The secret is to continue and to Know Thyself.

Action

1. What choices will you make to continue to court desire and activate your soul's purpose? Write them down. Pick one to work on this week.

2. In the section on Deeper Choices, we talked about bringing your daily life closer to your purpose by looking at arcs. What is your long arc? Are you aware of it? Can you write it down in general or specific form? Try one paragraph first. Whittle that down to a sentence. Can you state it simply in just one or two words? How will the arc of your coming year support this long arc? How will it be supported by it? Write three specific goals; then look at how your weekly and daily life may need to adjust to support these goals. Write out smaller daily or weekly goals that will be imbued by your soul's work.

3. Look over your accomplishments for the last six to twelve months. Do something to celebrate.

Chapter 10

THE OUTCOME
OF DESIRE

*It is not death that a man should fear, but he should fear
never beginning to live.*

Marcus Aurelius

We cannot know the outcome of desire. All we can do is live it.

Acknowledging this important truth frees us toward action.
It is our constant wanting to know how everything will turn out,
to avoid mistakes, to avoid hurting anyone or anything around us
that keeps us immobile, trapped in mediocrity and fear. We have
worked your way this far. We have examined thought and motiva-
tion. We have engaged and risked and sat again in silence. Now is
the place in the cycle simply to live. How will we walk with desire
and purpose? What will you commit to every day? There is nothing that can stop us when we recognize that obstacles are part of
the path as well.

Years ago, a dervish friend related something said to him by a
teacher when he was at a point of needing to change his life and
his relationship to love, work, and success. This teacher said: "The
ordinary person goes over the mountain. The Sufi goes through
the mountain."

The image of going through the mountain is not, for me, one of destruction of the mountain. Rather, it is the deep sense that *our lives are one with the mountain* and therefore all parts of ourselves are part of the mountain. Therefore, there is no impediment in our way. There is no other side. There is only self as mountain and mountain as self. All of the obstacles we perceive are also part of the divine flow; their molecules build and breakdown with our own. The deeper reality pointed to by mystics and physicists alike tells us this: we are united with everything. If we hold this as true, what is left to stop us?

We wake up in the morning and decide for ourselves: act or do not act. Choose or have choice forced upon us. Live our lives or succumb to passive choices by default. Going through the mountain requires the coming together of several things: practice; commitment; the strength of desire; and the knowledge that we are all made of the same stuff as the mountain itself.

We can become one with our obstacles. Compete with them if that fires up your will and determination. Soften around them if that helps you access compassion and enter the larger flow. In the *Bhagavad Gita*, when Arjuna quailed at doing his duty on the field of battle, Krishna enjoined him to become one with his duty, to become the avatar of his own destiny. Krishna could just as easily have reminded Arjuna that there was no separation between life and death, between cousin and brother and friend.[35] The forces had to come together, somehow. What Arjuna needed was not to find obstacles in front of him, but rather to find union and mastery within.

---

35. My favorite translation of the *Bhagavad Gita* is by Barbara Stoller Miller (Bantam, 1986).

WORTHWHILE RISKS

We won't lie. The decision to become visible is a risk.
CHRIS BROGAN AND JULIEN SMITH

Taking risks by making ourselves visible can feel hard. But not acting because we fear this visibility is worse. We have put ourselves out there, followed the dream, taken the stand, and shown up because it was right and necessary. Then someone takes a pot-shot at us, undermines us, talks trash about us. There will always be someone who does this.

In order to be criticized for what we've done, we have to be willing to do something. Sometimes the continued activation of our true will in the world can feel difficult, because it means we fly above the radar where there is no longer as much room to hide from ourselves and others. This is true whether we end up in the larger public eye, step forward within a small community of friends, submit a poem for publication, or tell someone we love them.

Fear of exposure and censure is often the bane of work on scales both small and large. We grow tired of scrutiny, or shy away from even the idea of scrutiny. We ourselves complain about other people's projects and have to field complaints about our own. There are two facets of this that interest me.

First, when I am offering criticism of other people's projects, it isn't just a matter of good form that makes me think of something to compliment them on in order to bracket the critique. What is more deeply important is that I *have to realize the risk and effort required for them to have put the project together at all.* If I can start with that, my view changes immediately. This then enables my critique to offer more valid information. Truly, something in me needs to applaud the chutzpah and will necessary to have dreamed the dream, nailed the boards together, built the coalition, organized the event, written the book, planted the garden, or raised the child.

This attitudinal shift changes something that connects me more deeply to my core and broadens my vision of what it is I am facing that I wish were different. This applies in multiple situations and with many people: at work, at home, among friends, with public figures, with artists, with politicians, with committee members. If I can access my frustration *after* I acknowledge an appreciation of people sticking their necks out, I bring both power and compassion to my response. That is always a good thing. It also serves to shift mere carping and complaining toward actual criticism that may help me or someone else to learn something different.

Second, this shift also helps me when I turn the lens on my own life and work. I become able to recognize that going through all of the Four Powers to manifest something takes courage and patience. I can better assess criticism that comes my way, taking in what feels helpful or accurate and letting the rest go. I can realize it is usually not about me, but about the person critiquing. My ability to be in the flow of creation is strengthened by this, and that helps me to continue to do my Divine Work in the world.

PERFECTIONISM

In order to go on living one must try to escape the death involved in perfectionism.

HANNAH ARENDT

Why do we undermine ourselves? Because we want to be perfect. Why is perfectionism a form of death? Because for something to be perfect, it must remain static, frozen in time. Perfectionism kills creativity before we begin and, once begun, keeps us from finishing, because we know that nothing is ever really finished. We fear that, if we seal the canvas, type the last word, or step off the committee, we are saying the work is complete and therefore must be perfect.

Thinking that things have to be exactly a certain way or be counted as failures attaches too much importance to the outcome rather than the process; it ties our life energy up into knots, often with the help of thoughts and emotions. When we are worried about what people will think or whether we're good enough, we are not moving from our core desires, nor are we daring to enact our will. We are allowing fear to dictate our growth and our learning. When we do this, we end up smaller and less rich than is possible.

In order to enter the creative phase of manifestation, we have to be willing to risk censure, derision, and even applause. We have to be willing to be seen. To help turn energy toward greater flights of daring, remember what we just said about worthwhile risks. To dare, make an internal turn. Whenever you start to criticize someone—including yourself—first pause and thank them for showing up to try.

We can do our best, and know that perfection is a process—changeable and gorgeous as the movement from seed to plant to flower to fruit to compost to seed.

Soul Support

Get a favorite cup and put a couple of inches of fresh water into it. Hold in your mind whatever ties you up in knots. Find your center and your edge, your circumference. Breathe deeply.

Imagine that, as you breathe, you are filled with more and more light and life. Hold your hands over the cup of water. Imagine the light and life filling you up and "pushing" what has been knotted up down your arms, out of your hands, and into the water. Keep breathing in life, and exhaling what needs releasing. Eventually, life and light will move out from your hands into the water, charging it up with possibility and change. Know that the cup is filled with water, with that which was bound in you, and with light and life. Breathe out a blessing upon the water. Then drink it down.

What was in knots is now free and moving through you in a new form, carrying a blessing for the work that is yet to come.

Repeat this as many times as you like, knowing that, with this freed-up energy, you can make the changes necessary to manifest desire and live more fully. This is the rite of unbinding the life force. Over time, it has the power to heal your most pernicious wounds.[36]

INTEGRATION

I see how we struggle, the patterns we repeat over and over again. And I ask myself: What will it take for us to want liberation more than anything? What will it take for us to seek to balance love and power? What will it take for us to stop selling ourselves short and

---

36. This cleansing exercise comes in different forms and is known by several names, including "Kala" and "The Rite of Unbinding." For more information and other ways to do this, please see my books *Evolutionary Witchcraft* (Tarcher/Penguin, 2005) and *Kissing the Limitless* (Weiser Books, 2009). I give thanks to my teachers for the blessing of this rite.

start lifting each other up? What will it take for us to set aside the waters of forgetfulness and take up the cup of truth?

What attracts you that is deadening? What do you think you want that saps your life energy and individuality? What keeps you small, controllable, making choices that don't serve you or your friends or even this earth? Look around. The shiny attractiveness of advertising and our consumer culture has convinced us to walk into a tragic, toxic mess. The lure of false power rips apart our communities. Even those who fight against this are not immune.

What is important to us? I'm talking here culturally and spiritually. Do we want some modicum of social equity in our subcultures? Do we fight each other for recognition and to ensure that our sense of entitlement is justified? Do we think we are too small and ordinary to have much effect? Do we tear each other down? Do we diminish our own talents, wishes, and will?

We can pledge to make a greater attempt: to temper impatience with compassion; to think generously rather than to give way to constriction; to push ourselves to live well, with heart and with soul.

The earth needs us. The cosmos needs us. Art needs us. Love needs us. Beauty needs us. Courage needs us. Let us help each other. Let us shout "Wake up!" from the rooftops. Let us dance.

Soul Support

You can be more than you think you are now. You can access all the stages of your development in every moment—including being at your very best and brightest—and integrate them into a whole that is larger than its parts. Will you call up the parts that are scared to live at full capacity or the parts that want to numb you back to a more comfortable size? Will you call up the parts that are generous, or the parts that wish to feel grander and more deserving than others? Will you support your best work and the best work of your community? Or will you drown within a solipsistic sea?

Take a breath. Find your center and your circumference. Find that in you which wants to live life to the utmost. Let this impulse bolster the parts that may still feel afraid. Breathe love into fear. Breathe compassion into unworthiness. Breathe hope into anger. Breathe courage into doubt. Breath in life. Breathe out connection. Breathe up a prayer to your own divine nature. Notice how you feel.

ACTIVATING YOUR LIFE

Living our destiny includes our whole lives. Lifting steel and iron is an act of prayer. Slicing a tomato is an act of sex. Sitting in meditation is an act of love. Sharing a beloved kiss is an act of will. What will it take for us to realize this fully, in every cell of our Being? What will it take for us to activate our lives?

Manifestation requires integration at every step along the path. It is not enough to let the parts that know, know, or the parts that act, act. We have to find the ways in which things are still not fitting together and the ways in which some things are being left out.

Here is an example from my life:

Once, my trainer challenged me by asking me to examine what importance I placed on my physical work versus my other work. This brought me up short. I strive toward integration. As an intellectual, I have worked hard to be physical and emotional.

Still, I knew deep inside that I was failing to embrace my body fully. Workouts were still something I "made time for" rather than seeing as simply another necessary part of my spiritual life, my Great Work, and my practice. I still thought that going to the gym was something I did before the rest of my day started, rather than something that contributed to the larger arc.

This challenge was a good example of why I often say that we all need teachers. Good teachers catch the blind spots we so assiduously avoid. I was still defaulting into "I should work out" because, deep down, it is not my first impulse. So I ended up thinking that I needed to engage will and fight against sloth. But that is not the relationship I seek. I seek to listen to and ask my body what it truly needs. I do this with food. I can do this on the road when my body really wants movement because of sitting on airplanes. Putting some movement into my classes is second nature to me, as is riding my bike and walking. Yet, not listening happens when habit takes over, and sometimes will becomes force. Sometimes rest is what is necessary. So listening becomes the practice once again.

I ask a lot of myself and a lot of my students and clients. I want to ask even more: for a deeper awareness that the separation we enact is false; for a realization that engaging the body, at whatever level and ability we can, is just like listening to guides or meditating or writing or making good food. It is not something to be "fit in." Self-care is soul care.

Soul Support

Magic makes each moment.

The light is inside you. Let the fresh wind move through your mind, body, and soul. Let it clear you of the sleep of your

MAKE MAGIC OF YOUR LIFE

own making. Do not shy away from darkness, but neither shrink from brilliant dawn. Desire is encoded in your heart. Desire walks with you every step of the way. Desire is in despair. Desire is held in sadness. Desire is only absent in pure joy, for in pure joy is the force of desire met with the fullness of your life.

Let yourself seek; then let yourself feel satisfied. But do not let the satisfaction stay for long. Desire is the calling forward of your life back into motion. Can you hear it? Can you feel it? Let it tug at you, as it whispers to you: "Go!" Open the soles of your feet and the crown of your head. Say this prayer:

I commit to living life out loud, and to seeking out silence. I commit to reaching fully, earth to sky. I commit to Love. I commit to Will.

THE POWER OF CHANGE

I often say that God Hirself is in process. One thing that can hang us up at any stage in this work is forgetting that all things change. Even after all of this self-examination, daring, and soul work, some still feel that the soul's work has to be some big, earth-shattering, unchangeable thing. This isn't how it works out for most of us. We figure out our purpose by living; our lives shift according to our purpose, and our purpose shifts according to our lives.

At a workshop, Terri insisted that she didn't really have soul work. She then went on to describe all the ways in which she "just" did one thing or another. My jaw, and the jaws of the other workshop participants, literally dropped. As she spoke, Terri painted a coherent picture of how she served the world. In every scenario, she listened, she extracted information on how best to assist the people involved, she acted herself, and she helped *them* act in order to get their needs met. Since this was what she had always done, she didn't realize it was her work! It felt ordinary.

Most often, it does. My work feels ordinary to me. I know a cinematographer whose work feels ordinary to him. I know activists, parents, teachers, firefighters, nurses, and musicians who all simply do the work in front of them. Most of these people have a calling. Most of them also live pretty "ordinary" lives.

This grounding in the ordinary enables us to remain flexible and to follow the course of desire as that mighty river runs through our lives. People often ask me how I've built my career. I didn't. I was just following the tugging of desire at every turn. How it manifested changed over time. It looks the way it looks right now—for now. It will likely change again. As soon as life starts to feel too special, the pressure can grow so intense that we become performers on a stage rather than living out our deepest calling. We think we need to keep up appearances. We stop learning readily or easily. We grow more and more afraid to fail.

When we go through phases where we feel we have lost the thread of desire, the pressure toward perfection becomes crippling. Embracing change is the antidote to this. Things do sometimes plateau. Sometimes we have less clarity. Remember compassion? Remember the stillness at your core? You can connect to both, recognizing that even loss of connection to desire is another portion of your soul's journey.

Look back on the ordinary heroes I wrote about in chapter 2; review the words of our Wise Council that grace each part opening. These people live extraordinary lives without having lost touch with all the ways in which life is also simple. They make music and raise children. They save lives and go camping. They inspire others and wash the dishes. We all can manifest lives that simultaneously feel ordinary and extraordinary. This opens us up to the most powerful magic of all—gratitude.

Don't grow brittle. Encourage flexibility. Don't be afraid of change. Count your blessings as they come. This journey doesn't end until we choose to give up. In a world of change, there is no need for despair. Something new will always come along.

GETTING BIGGER

The more we allow ourselves to feel the beauty of desire as it moves through our lives, the more we need room to live a little bit bigger, a little bit bolder, with access to more and more energy. Remember the exercise of finding your center and circumference and then allowing an exhalation to push your edges outward? There will come times in this quest to manifest your Divine Work when your edges will indeed be pushed. If you can use your powers of observation and notice what is occurring, you become well placed to expand further, rather than retreating or contracting.

Most people will have at least a moment, if not a few days or even a month, when they fight against the expansion. It helps me to remember that this is another way that my ego tells me it feels afraid. It is fine to feel afraid. Allow yourself to write about it, sing about it, dance it out, schedule time to complain to a friend about all the reasons you don't want to be bigger, brighter, and more visible—all the ways in which you want to avoid greater responsibility or risk. Thrash around a bit. Then use that energy to expand again, to root deeper in the earth and reach higher toward the sky.

Sometimes this may not look or feel graceful. That is also alright. Think of an adolescent having a growing spurt; we are doing the same. Calling upon compassion serves us in these moments.

Opening our hearts reminds us that perfection is not static, but moves and changes as we move and change.

Our egos may also feel uncomfortable with expansion because we think we should not take up too much space. It is not always clear, however, what "too much space" is. What I always tell my students and clients who are going through this process is that, the more connected we are to our center and our circumference, the more smoothly we can operate in the world at full power. Those who have worked hard to expand their capacity to live powerfully and with love may come to yet another threshold where they are called upon to expand and deepen yet again.

Soul Support

Think of some big things that are beautiful and take up just the right amount of space. Humpback whales. The moon. Sycamore trees. Gas giants. The Sierra Mountains. The Atlantic Ocean. African elephants. Manatees.

Think of some "larger-than-life" humans. What about them inspires you? What repels you? What captures your interest? Which of these people do you imagine has a strong connection to their physical and spiritual cores? Why do you get this impression? Which ones do you imagine aren't that well connected? What accounts for this difference?

Imagine what your life would be like if you felt less frightened, or more certain. Imagine what your life would be like if you took up the amount of space your soul is longing for and did so from the center to the very edges of your Being.

What will help support you in this growth? Can you nurture that?

Expand the size of your core—that place that sits between your navel and pelvis. Imagine that it grows as bright as the sun. Let your Being radiate outward, communicating with everyone around you, from the smallest insect to the farthest star being born.

SERVICE AND PURPOSE

I may work hard, but so do all the men and women I met in Afghanistan who have much less in terms of opportunity or material wealth. What comes to me does so at least partly through forces outside of my control. My privilege and my responsibility, therefore, is to appreciate what I have, to manage these resources wisely, and in the best interests of all.

MARIANNE ELLIOTT[37]

In the course of writing this book, I was asked how best to align our lives so the fulfillment of personal desire would increase love and work with family and community. I loved that question, feeling that its implications were huge. I sat with it for a long time.

Here is the beginning of an answer.

For me, what connects desire with community is service. When I engage in overt acts of service, I reconnect to my purpose through an intense feeling of gratitude. I am placed in front of my privilege and see so clearly all the ways in which my life is blessed. Working to serve the homeless and working poor of San Francisco or helping a grieving family fight for justice not only brings

---

37. From her memoir *Zen Under Fire*, which will be available outside of New Zealand by summer 2013. For information, see *www.marianne-elliott.com*.

my body, mind, heart, and soul to worthy tasks, but also allows me to see firsthand how deeply amazing my life is.

Why is this important? The more often we can feel grateful for blessed gifts, the more this energy expands to flow outward through our lives and all our work. In my life, I recognize that cleaning giant soup pots or showing up at a city council meeting are just as important as teaching 200 people how to align their souls. One is not separate from the other. Each feeds into the next. When giving an unwashed drug addict a hug he just won't get from anyone else, my humanity confronts the humanity of another, and all of a sudden, my every word and action have more meaning and resonance. I recognize that everything I do, everything we do, matters.

Service also provides the clear ability to see how doing the Work of This God or enacting our life purpose is *in itself* an act of service. Until we feel in our bones what service—particularly joyous service—is, it is hard to see just how the work we are called to do serves. The work we are called to do may feel simple and ordinary. We've talked about this in earlier chapters. I'm here to tell you that this does not matter. You may "only" drive a group of kids to soccer practice. But if you do so with love—listening to their stories with interest, offering comfort or advice when needed—you just may be changing someone's life forever. That may be your Divine Work, and it certainly serves those children far beyond the simple act of driving.

When we think of our purpose, our divine mandate, as something that facilitates acts of service, this frees us up to do what we are meant to do. Our souls' light will shine more brightly if we let go of yet another round of expectations and allow ourselves simply to live as we are—knowing that, every day, we are following the path of desire home, and that home includes the multiverse. Home includes Afghani women, old-growth forests, children in Detroit, your family, the ozone, and you.

How can we not serve that? How can that service not be our deeper purpose? Every painting we make, every poem we write, every house we erect, every elder we care for, every patch of kale we plant serves and builds and becomes our life purpose.

When we remember that we cocreate our lives, our communities, and the world, we are returned again and again to the fabric of All. God Hirself shines within us—a beacon and a blessing.

We become, finally, the change we want to see in the world.[38]

Soul Support

The gift the cosmos gives you is the gift you give the world. Your life is a shining beacon of hope to us all. There is nothing you cannot do to support the deepest desire of your soul.

When you walk as someone fully manifesting your Divine Work in the world, the world opens to you. Life will still have challenges, but you will find more support than you even knew was possible. You will seek out help, inspiration, and joy. Doesn't your soul deserve this gift? I think it does. Not only that, but once you open to the gift being offered, the gifts you yourself pass on increase. Every moment becomes another opportunity to serve, to love, and to shine.

---

38. I, of course, paraphrase the great teacher and activist Mahatma Gandhi: "You must be the change you wish to see in the world."

Let yourself open to the flow of generous creativity, knowing that in receiving this, you gain the ability to offer something fine, something strong, and something beautiful.

Action

1. How are you feeling about desire, purpose, and manifestation? Do you feel excitement, satisfaction, resistance, shyness, fear, or something else? Notice if there are portions of your work that you feel ready to revisit or take to a deeper level. Sit with yourself awhile and listen for what will best support the opening of your purpose and the following or fulfillment of your desire. Let yourself do this work. Give yourself the gift of staying with it.

2. Seek out inspiration from yourself and your friends, from Nature, art, and music, and from the kindness of strangers. This will help to counter fear and worry. It is the water needed for your journey. Add inspirational things to your altar. Make an inspirational playlist. Go to an art gallery or the farmer's market. See a movie. Have some friends over for tea and conversation. Pray. Look. Listen. Then go.

PART VI

DESIRE'S END, DESIRE'S BEGINNING

AS THE RIVER FLOWS ON, WE ASK THE WISE COUNCIL:

WHAT MOST HELPS YOU TO FOLLOW THE COURSE OF DESIRE?

Listening to my body and what it has to say to me. Strong emotional feelings tend to provoke strong physical reactions within me. When I feel a strong and unusual sensation, I know that there's something here that I need to investigate.

ANAAR

I usually respond to a desire to create words from experiences that can feel wordless; first to create a kind of order for myself, and then, hopefully, for others. The supernatural stories I write are metaphors for the real-life horrors and losses all of us must face.

TANANARIVE DUE

In following the course of desire it allows me to open myself to the infinite possibilities that come from identifying what my passions are. Living a life of passion fuels my ability to do my best, create my goals, identify desires and pursue a stronger connection with myself and my version of divinity. I connect with a source of my desire to be a part of the solution for social injustices by educating myself and advocating for the dreams of others. The very opportunity to do this is a part of what helps me to continue.

CRYSTAL BLANTON

There is always this inner drive to keep creating and looking for new ways to express myself through music or supporting others who are creative through music. If I ignore it, it always comes back and urges me on. It hasn't stopped yet.

DANA REASON

Chapter 11

THE GREAT RETURN

For behold, I have been with you from the beginning, and I
am that which is attained at the end of desire.

FROM *THE CHARGE OF THE GODDESS*[39]

We began in chapter 0 with God Hirself creating the cosmos from the seeds of desire. There was a desire to know, to touch, to look, to differentiate. We read about the ancient Greeks and the power of *eros*, the power of desire, tugging us back toward the source. We can pause now, take a breath, and know that our souls' work, no matter how it manifests in the world, is at its core this Great Return. We return to source and are part of source, simultaneously. That is the mystery that is ever unfolding within and around us.

We have a center and a circumference that both connect us to the limitless whole and differentiate us from it. Our cells have walls that enable them to do their particular work, and yet they are part of the larger being we call ourselves. We are the same

---

39. Written by Doreen Valiente, drawing upon source materials from Charles Leland and Aleister Crowley. It has been adapted by Starhawk and many others and is available in various sources.

within the cosmic flow. Our destiny is to find our work and, in doing so, rejoin the greater work of the cosmos itself. Our souls' work is both specific and grand, ordinary and sublime. Our lives are sacred.

What does it mean for the sacred to say: "I am that which is attained at the end of desire"? Desire is what continuously connects us to the sacred pattern, the pathway that gives our lives meaning and purpose. All of the listening and risking serves something far greater than our individual lives. We become one with the flow of divinity. We become one with ourselves.

If the sacred is with us from the beginning and is attained at the end of desire, does this not point to the pull and push of *eros* I spoke of in the opening chapter? The Great Return is always filled with life, love, sex, and some desire. Everything in the cosmos is involved in this activity.

The truth is that there is nothing to be attained and no end to desiring. There is only a life lived in truth and beauty, with compassion and strength—a life that keeps diving back into the river of desire, following its course. When we enter desire, we find God Hirself waiting.

THE RITUAL OF MANIFESTATION

For this ritual, you will need to remember everything that you opened, called in, and gathered to yourself from the Rituals of Knowing, Willing, Daring, and Keeping Silence. Your place of power—your sacred place—is always with you. Feel how you reach between earth and sky. Take a full breath. Claim this space. Know that you have access to your own divinity, to the Four Powers of the Sphinx, and to the love and expansiveness of God Hirself.

Regardless of where you are in this process, you can do some specific work to manifest your heart's desire and your soul's purpose right now. There comes a time, whether you believe you are ready or not, when you just need to do something. Manifestation is served by doing. It is not thinking or dreaming. It uses the energy and intention of your previous work and it *moves*. The part of your soul that is connected to the nonverbal and instinctive needs to be engaged now. I sometimes call this the animal soul. It needs something to hold on to when the human, rational soul starts changing mental habits—while the divine part of self, the God Soul, is connecting up with the macrocosm and your destiny.[40]

This is where physical prayer comes to our aid. Prayer that engages the physical and the senses draws all three parts of the soul together. The tactile, sensory component captures the attention of the animal soul, and the rational soul helps to keep our intention clear and at the forefront. This is how our God Soul reminds us that we are connected to the limitless flow and therefore have all that we need to manifest what our hearts and souls desire.

Do this work as a series of steps that will take you through all the Four Powers in turn.

First, invoke the power To Know. Do some writing and set a clear intention. What do you want to manifest at this time? What support does your soul require? Be as specific as you can be, but also allow room for the universe to work. For example, if your prayer is to know your soul's work truly, write something like this:

---

40. For more information on how I work with the parts of the soul, see *Evolutionary Witchcraft* (Tarcher/Penguin, 2005). Another resource is *Etheric Anatomy* by Victor and Cora Anderson (Acorn Guild Press, 2004).

I wish to know what my true work in the world is. I wish to be healthy and happy in my pursuit of what it is that I can manifest. I wish to be well supported as I learn. I am open to good guidance.

If you feel your soul's work is to be a concert pianist, the intention woven into your prayer may look like this:

It is my desire to serve the world by spreading beauty. May my music open the hearts and souls of whoever hears me play. May the universe open the way for my music to touch the right people, supporting their healing and awakening and supporting my life financially and artistically.

Notice that both intentions have specific wants and needs included, and yet are not so specific as to leave no room for destiny to flow as it will. Ground the grand in the specific—your vision needs that as a foundation—but don't pin it down so tightly that there is no room for grace to meet desire. Grace is the unexpected that arrives when you have prepared, yet remain open.

THE SPELL: PART TWO

Get a candle in a color, size, and shape that best appeals to your animal soul. For our purposes, it is best not to have a candle in a jar, although it can be placed in a jar later. Is the right color royal blue or red? Green or yellow? Or perhaps no color at all? Does the candle smell of beeswax or some other scent? If it is unscented and you aren't allergic, you may wish to gather some essential oils that appeal to you in order to anoint the candle. What are the right ones for this working? Let your soul decide. To what are you drawn? What feels right? Make sure that both the candle and any oil you choose reflect your will and intention.

Pick a day or night when you won't be disturbed. Traditionally, this should be done somewhere between the waxing gibbous and full moons, as a sign that energy is strengthening. Gather a pin or needle—the feather of a bird or the quill of a porcupine or a small knife can be used instead—your candle, a holder, and some oil. Make sure you have some quiet. Shower or bathe. Read over what you wrote in the first part of the spell. Ask yourself: "Is this my Will?" If the answer is still yes, proceed.

Slow down your breathing. Take in one breath to honor your physical body. Take in one breath to honor your animal soul. Take in one breath to honor your rational soul. Take in one breath to honor your God Soul. Exhale that last breath up, and then imagine your connection to your center. If there are any specific deities or allies you wish to ask for help, invite them to join you.

You are ready. Using your pin or whatever tool you have chosen, carve some of the words from your intention into the candle. If you have oil, rub it on the candle, motioning toward yourself. Keep your will and intention in mind. Imagine you are drawing the prayer toward you.

Holding the candle in your hands, say out loud the words of your intention. What do you wish to manifest? Breathe in life and exhale that toward the candle, breathing across the wax and the carved words. Do this until it feels right. Then place the candle in whatever holder you have. If you have also written out your intention nicely on a piece of paper, place it beneath the candle holder. If you don't want anyone else to be able to read it, fold it. Find your still center once again.

Say out loud:

With the power of Daring, I light the flame of my heart's desire, bringing light and warmth to the work of my soul.

Light the candle. Then sit with the power To Keep Silence and breathe. Feel your center and your circumference and, holding awareness of them simultaneously, gaze upon the flame. Let your whole Being begin to vibrate with the flame, tuning to this prayer you are making.

Sit until the ritual feels complete for the moment; then extinguish the candle.

THE SPELL: PART THREE

Work with your candle once a day. Light the candle, restate your intention, and sit in meditation. Do this until it has burned all the way down. If any wax is left after the wick is gone, you can melt it down and carry it with you or save it for the next time you have a fire and offer it to the larger flames, knowing that your life is always an offering to the greater whole. Dispose of any vestiges with the same clear intention you used to begin this working.

Live. Repeat your work with the Four Powers as often as it feels necessary. Remember, this is a cycle that never needs to feel complete. There is always some new insight or revelation, and some new source of support that will come your way, as long as you remain engaged.

Soul Support

Are you not part of God Hirself? Are you not an integral part of creation and the unfolding of the patterns of life? Why are you here? You are here to find and follow your destiny. You are here to listen to desire. Even if the call is faint, you can pray. Every time you show up to another friendship, you are seeking to follow the path of desire. Every time you go to another workshop, ritual, art gallery, concert, forest, or beach, you are seeking desire. To seek desire is to follow desire. What connects you? What draws you forward? What brings you back to relationship, again and again?

Desire is the fire beneath you that keeps you moving forward. Desire is the fire at sex and heart that illuminates your life. Desire is the sparking of the mind that spurs your thoughts toward creation. Desire flames in the cauldron of your belly, giving you the will to carry on.

GUIDED BY DESIRE

Power without love is reckless and abusive, and love without power is sentimental and anemic.

MARTIN LUTHER KING JR.

The people I love most in life are guided by desire. They listen to their God Souls and this tugging force of destiny. They light up themselves and the world around them in ways that may seem simple and basic, but that are driven by deep choice. And some of my friends? They set the world on fire.

What is your way? Are you still dousing the fires of desire with self-loathing or indecision? Are you sinking in and training in order to live a life that feels bold? Are you listening to the great silences and coming forth renewed? Are you speaking to the wind and to the rain? Desire draws all things together and draws still others on their way. Each peptide in your body forms itself to do its work. What is your work? These things that help you To Know, and To Will and To Dare, these things that rise from the power To Keep Silence—all of these are also part of the flowing of desire. Let yourself feel it. Let yourself taste it. Let yourself live.

The journey is moving ever onward. The process is never someday, but always now.

May your work be blessed. May your work be a blessing.

Fiat LVX.

GRATITUDE

No book is written in a vacuum. A lifetime of spiritual training and seeking has led me here, and many people and beings have helped me along the way. I offer thanks as always to my teachers, clients, students, and dear friends. I give thanks to everyone who took my Courting Desire class and the Temple of Love and Desire workshops, and to those who engaged with questions on Facebook, Twitter, and my blog on many of the topics in this book.

Particular thanks go to Jonathan and Robert for love, passion, insight, laughter, support, and home. Thanks to Samara for unexpected joy and to Carey Rockland, my former trainer, for kicking my ass. I'm much better for it.

Thanks as well to everyone who labors so hard at Weiser Books. I feel grateful for your continued support. This includes but is not limited to: Caroline, Amber, Laurie, Dennis, Jan, Jim, Bonni, Pat, and Kat. Thank you to Rynn Fox and Crow Walker for being excellent first readers and to Kaye for helping me with bookings so I can do things like write. Deep thanks to the Wise Council for sharing insight and experience. Gratitude and blessings to independent bookstores as well, particularly Fields Books and Treadwells.

Thanks to my Gods, Guides, and the ever present Lux, and to the limitless flow of God Hirself.

May all beings be blessed. May justice be realized.

EPILOGUE

WE ASK THE WISE COUNCIL:

DO YOU HAVE ANY LAST THOUGHTS ABOUT COURTING DESIRE?

Hindu scriptures are filled with many stories of saints, sages, and other great people tempted off a desired course. Some courted another desire, some kept their original desire. It's about the balance between various opportunities, wishes, and paths in life, and the result is what we do and who we become. A fascinating tale that has been going on since existence.

MIHIR MEGHANI

My first inclination is to say that I have followed my gut instincts all my life and this has led me into some distinct and wonderful places and many times I didn't know why I was following a particular thread. In the last five to ten years I've realized every thread I have followed has become a part of my work in the world. It has been my job to find a powerful synthesis of all these threads to create something that has never been created before. This is scary but ultimately satisfying. There is an idea in some schools of yoga and Buddhism that desire leads to suffering, but it can also become the seed of our service, our healing, our art. The trick is in learning to ride the tiger of my passions.

SUZANNE STERLING

For YEARS I let smart people talk me into things that just weren't right for me. I'll bet you have, too. I went down wrong paths, doing things I wasn't excited about, because someone or something convinced me it was what I "should" be doing. Then I finally figured out something that's made all the difference, and I've been happier and more successful since: There's a compass in your gut that points two directions: EXCITING and DRAINING. No matter what advice anyone gives you—no matter how smart the person telling you what to do—you need to let this compass override your other decisions. Whatever excites you, go do it. Whatever drains you, stop doing it.

DEREK SIVERS

The journey is not over. The creative and musical fire continues to burn in my belly, and it is too hot to burn itself out.

DANA REASON

MAKE MAGIC OF YOUR LIFE

ABOUT THE WISE COUNCIL

ANAAR

Anaar is a Grandmaster of the Anderson Feri tradition, as well as a priestess, dancer, artist, and costume designer. Her traveling boutique, Tombo Studio, was established in 1995. She says: "In my work as a designer I strive toward two quests. The first quest is for great design. The second, superb craftsmanship." She holds a degree in fine arts, and an MA in Arts and Consciousness. Anaar taught art in California prisons for many years and now makes her living as a performer and designer. One hallmark of her work is that every piece—whether performance, painting, or clothing— is done as an act of devotion.

Anaar teaches and performs internationally, and her work is featured in the Textile Research Centre in Leiden. She has also produced a dance DVD called *Dark Imaginations*. Find out more at *www.anaar.info* and *www.tombostudio.com*.

CRYSTAL BLANTON

Crystal Blanton is a Wiccan High Priestess living in the San Francisco Bay Area. She is a California native living in the heart of many of the Neo-Pagan movements. As a mother of four, grandmother of three, and a wife of thirteen years, she has experienced the ups and downs of family life and grown spiritually as a result. Professionally, Crystal has worked in social services for the last twelve years, specializing in addiction studies and counseling.

Crystal currently works as a drug and alcohol counselor in adolescent treatment while maintaining her family, mentoring students, running her personal business, being in a local coven, maintaining two traditions, and continuing to write for her community. Her first book, *Bridging the Gap*, was published in 2010 by Megalithic/Immanion Press. She is also featured in the anthology *Shades of Faith*. Find out more at *www.crystalblanton.com*.

TANANARIVE DUE

Tananarive Due teaches writing at Antioch University Los Angeles and holds the Cosby Chair in the Humanities at Spelman College (2012–13), where she teaches screenwriting and journalism. An American Book Award winner and NAACP Image Award recipient, she is the author of twelve novels that include *My Soul to Take*, *The Good House*, and the *Tennyson Hardwick* mystery series. She also wrote *The Black Rose*, a historical novel about the life of Madam C. J. Walker, and *Freedom in the Family: A Mother-Daughter Memoir of the Fight for Civil Rights*, which she coauthored with her mother, the late Civil Rights activist Patricia Stephens Due. *Freedom in the Family* was named 2003's Best Civil Rights Memoir by *Black Issues Book Review*.

Tananarive has been inducted into the Medill School of Journalism's Hall of Achievement at Northwestern University and received the New Voice in Literature Award at the Yari Yari

Pamberi conference cosponsored by New York University's Institute of African-American Affairs and African Studies Program and the Organization of Women Writers of Africa. She lives in the Atlanta area with her husband, author Steven Barnes, and their son, Jason. Find out more at *www.tananarivedue.com* and *www.tananarivedue.wordpress.com*.

JENNIFER LOUDEN

Jennifer Louden is the best-selling author of *The Woman's Comfort Book, The Couple's Comfort Book, The Pregnant Woman's Comfort Book, The Woman's Retreat Book,* and *Comfort Secrets for Busy Women.* She is a personal coach, a social commentator, and a cultural visionary. Her books have been translated into nine languages and have been bestsellers in both Germany and the U.S., reaching hundreds of thousands of women. Jennifer has taught her lively workshops and delivered her humorous and motivational keynotes across the U.S., Canada, and Europe at hospitals, women's health centers, corporations, and universities.

Jennifer has been featured in major publications and regularly shares her voice with an enthusiastic national audience. Her media appearances have included *The Oprah Show* and *Later Today,* and she has been featured on MSNBC, CNN, and Fit TV. Articles about her work have appeared in *Glamour, Shape, People, Redbook, Good Housekeeping, Self, New Woman, Ladies Home Journal, Yoga Journal, Health, InStyle,* and *Parents,* as well as in many local papers. She lives, savors, and serves on an island in Puget Sound. Find out more at *www.jenniferlouden.com*.

Mihir Meghani

Mihir Meghani is an emergency physician at Kaiser Permanente Hospital. He provided medical care in India after the 2001 earthquake, in New York after 9/11, and in Sri Lanka after the 2004 tsunami. He has also helped train Ukrainians in disaster management. A member of the U.S. Department of Homeland Security's Disaster Medical Assistance Team, his special interests are disaster medicine, international emergency medicine, medicine of developing countries, and the cultural and spiritual aspects of medicine.

Mihir has received numerous awards for his community service. He is involved in environmental causes in the San Francisco Bay Area, interfaith dialogue, rural development in India, youth education, and Indian and Hindu community activities. Mihir is founder and president of both the Hindu American Foundation and Democracies Against Terror. He also serves on the Board of the Silicon Valley Interreligious Council. Find out more at *www.permanente.net* and *www.hafsite.org*.

Dana Reason

Dana Reason is a Canadian-born pianist, composer, improviser, and musicologist. As a pianist, composer, and improviser, Dana has performed extensively throughout the U.S., Canada, and Europe, and can be heard on over eleven CD recordings. She has appeared at Frau Musica Nova, Banff Center For The Arts, Stanford University, San Francisco Jazz Festival, Spring Reverb, and Is That Jazz? Seattle Festival among others. Dana was part of The Space Between Trio with Pauline Oliveros in the 2000s. She has performed with Mark Dresser, Joelle Leandre, Lori Goldston, Bert

Turetzky, Alex Cline, Barre Philips, Fred Frith, Cecil Taylor, Lisle Ellis, George E. Lewis, and many others.

Dana is currently the director of Popular Music Studies at Oregon State University in the School of Arts and Communication. She is the founder and artistic director of Between the Cracks Forum: Music, Sound and Interactivity (2008–present)—a cross-disciplinary initiative designed to foster contemporary and creative music performance and development. She is also responsible for a new series for Improvised Music Practices at The Red Room At Interzone Café in Corvallis, Oregon. Find out more at *www.danareason.com*.

JOHN SEED

John Seed is an Australian environmentalist and director of the Rainforest Information Centre, which successfully campaigned to save the subtropical rain forests of New South Wales. A prominent figure in the deep ecology movement and cocreator of the Council of All Beings, he has taught worldwide. With Joanna Macy, Pat Fleming, and Professor Arne Naess, he wrote *Thinking Like a Mountain—Towards a Council of All Beings* (New Society Publishers), which has now been translated into ten languages.

In 1995, John was awarded the Order of Australia Medal (OAM) by the Australian government for services to conservation and the environment. He is a Fellow of the Findhorn Foundation and occasional Scholar-in-Residence at the Esalen Institute. Currently, he is working on tree-planting projects in India and Kenya, food security permaculture in Zimbabwe, and a Japanese language website working to protect Tasmanian forests. He continues to facilitate experiential deep ecology and climate change workshops around Australia. Find out more at *www.johnseed.net*.

Derek Sivers

Originally a professional musician and circus clown, Derek Sivers created CD Baby in 1998, helping to change the face of the music industry. It became the largest seller of independent music online, with $100 million in sales for 150,000 musicians. In 2008, Derek sold CD Baby for $22 million, giving the proceeds to a charitable trust for music education. He is a frequent speaker at the TED Conference, with over 5 million views of his talks. In 2011, he published a book, *Anything You Want,* which shot to #1 in all of its Amazon categories.

An entrepreneur, programmer, minimalist, leader, and avid student of life, Derek currently lives in Singapore, where he is creating his next company. Find out more at *www.sivers.org.*

Suzanne Sterling

Suzanne is an ecstatic vocalist, innovative composer, teacher, and invoker of the sacred. As both a performing and recording artist, as well as a facilitator of transformational workshops and intensives for many years, Suzanne has received critical acclaim. Called a contemporary "musical priestess," she creates sacred and participatory ceremonies for large gatherings and festivals worldwide. As a voice for joyful and sustainable activism, she has created trainings and curriculums for numerous communities, is cocreator of Off the Mat, Into the World® programs, and was cofounder of Bare Witness Humanitarian Tours.

Suzanne's musical explorations in the realm of electronic dance music, devotional chanting, and songs of the ecstatic soul have brought her to the forefront of the "kirtronica" sound. She has performed and toured internationally, both solo and with the well-known electronic dance act Medicine Drum, the innovative electronic dance act Alcyone (System Recordings NY), and the acoustic trio Kali's Angels. Her music has been commissioned for film, theater, and DVD. As well as performing, she facilitates retreats and workshops in the U.S. and abroad. Find out more at *www.suzannesterling.com*.

BIBLIOGRAPHY

Aristotle. *The Eudemian Ethics* (Oxford World's Classics). Oxford University Press, 2011.

Anderson, Cora. *In Mari's Bower: A Biography of Victor H. Anderson*. Marion Street Press, 2012.

Anderson, Victor H. *Etheric Anatomy: The Three Selves and Astral Travel*. Acorn Guild Press, 2004.

Arendt, Hannah. *The Life of the Mind*, vols. 1 and 2. Mariner Books, 1981.

Bayles, David, and Ted Orland. *Art and Fear: Observations on the Perils (and Rewards) of Artmaking*. Image Continuum Press, 2010.

Cooper, Rabbi David. *God Is a Verb: Kabbalah and the Practice of Mystical Judaism*. Riverhead, 1998.

Coyle, T. Thorn. *Evolutionary Witchcraft*. Tarcher/Penguin, 2005.

———. *Kissing the Limitless: Deep Magic and the Great Work of Transforming Yourself and the World*. Weiser Books, 2009.

Godin, Seth. *Graceful*. New Word City, 2010.

Lévi, Eliphas. *Transcendental Magic*. Kessinger Publishing, 1942. Later annotated editions are available.

Miller, Barbara Stoller. *The Bhagavad-Gita: Krishna's Counsel in Time of War*. Bantam Classics, reissued 1986.

Needleman, Jacob, ed. *The Inner Journey: Views from the Gurdjieff Work*. PARABOLA Anthology Series: Morning. Light Press, 2008.

AND AS ALWAYS:

The writings of Marcus Aurelius, Epictetus, and Mevlana Jalaluddin Rumi.

MAKE MAGIC OF YOUR LIFE

ABOUT THE AUTHOR

T. Thorn Coyle is a pagan, mystic, activist, and an internationally respected teacher and mentor on pagan subjects. She is the author of *Kissing the Limitless* and *Evolutionary Witchcraft*, hosts the Elemental Castings podcast series, writes a popular blog, *Know Thyself*, and has produced several CDs of sacred music.

Thorn works with Buddhists, Christians, Muslims, Jews, and Atheists on justice issues. She has spoken on homelessness and the death penalty in Catholic churches and led services at Sojourner Truth, the first African American Unitarian congregation in Washington, DC. Thorn has presented at the Parliament of the World's Religions and the National Covenant of Unitarian Universalist Pagans. She speaks at conferences and teaches workshops worldwide, and is a member of Spiritual Directors International.

She lives in the San Francisco Bay Area. Visit her at *www.thorncoyle.com.*